Parentology*

*Everything You Wanted to Know
about the Science of Raising Children
but Were Too Exhausted to Ask*

DALTON CONLEY

with E &

Yo Xing Heyno Augustus Eisner Alexander Weiser Knuckles Jeremijenko-Conley

Simon & Schuster Paperbacks

New York   London   Toronto   Sydney   New Delhi

Simon & Schuster Paperbacks
An Imprint of Simon & Schuster, Inc.
1230 Avenue of the Americas
New York, NY 10020

First Simon & Schuster trade paperback edition March 2015

SIMON & SCHUSTER PAPERBACKS and colophon are
registered trademarks of Simon & Schuster, Inc.

For information about special discounts for bulk purchases,
please contact Simon & Schuster Special Sales at
1-866-506-1949 or business@simonandschuster.com

The Simon & Schuster Speakers Bureau can bring authors to your live event.
For more information or to book an event contact the
Simon & Schuster Speakers Bureau at 1-866-248-3049
or visit our website at www.simonspeakers.com.

Designed by Ruth Lee-Mui
Jacket design by Laurie Carkeet
Jacket illustration by Shannon May

Manufactured in the United States of America

1   3   5   7   9   10   8   6   4   2

The Library of Congress has cataloged the hardcover edition as follows:

Conley, Dalton
Parentology : everything you wanted to know about the science of raising children
but were too exhausted to ask / Dalton Conley ; with E & Yo Xing Heyno
Augustus Eisner Alexander Weiser Knuckles Jeremijenko-Conley.
pages cm
Includes bibliographical references.
1. Conley, Dalton, 1969—Family. 2. Parenthood. 3. Child rearing. 4. Parenting.
I. Title.
HQ755.8.C6543 2014
649'—1dc23   2013024320

ISBN 978-1-4767-1265-9
ISBN 978-1-4767-1266-6 (pbk)
ISBN 978-1-4767-1267-3 (ebook)

To My Own Parental Units, Ellen and Steve:
What can I say? You tried your best.

Parentology 101 Syllabus

Preface: "Parentology" Defined

Parentology [pair-*uh*n-tol-*uh*-jee] [ipa: peər ən tɒl ə d͡ʒi] noun:

A philosophy of highly engaged child rearing in which one (A) accesses all relevant research; (B) makes a practice of constantly weighing said research against one's own experience and common sense; and (C) invents unique methodologies on the fly and fearlessly carries them out in order to test creative hypotheses about best practices for one's own particular offspring.

Like Mormonism and Jazz, Parentology is a uniquely American, improvisational approach to the raising of children. It relies on both modern science and old school intuition.

Related forms:

Parentologist: One who practices parentology.

Synonyms: Jazz parenting; post-Spock parenting; scientific American parenting

Antonyms: Old-world parenting; traditional parenting; textbook parenting; tiger mothering; bringing up bébé

Origin: 2014, portmanteau of "parenting" + "ology" (as in study of)

Parentology

1

What *Not* to Expect
When You're Expecting

"Everything our parents said was good is bad.
Sun, milk, red meat . . . college."
—Alvy Singer in *Annie Hall*

WHAT WOODY ALLEN claimed thirty-five years ago holds equally true today: parenting advice is always changing and often wrong. In 2014, milk is good again (the Dutch have the highest per capita dairy consumption and as a result are the tallest population on Earth and have the lowest rate of osteoporosis and hip fractures in old age)—unless of course you are one of the increasing ranks of the lactose or casein intolerant. Sun is also good again, since one of the theories du jour is that we collectively suffer from a vitamin D deficit and seasonal affective disorder. But too much sun is bad if you are skin type one (i.e. pasty white). Meanwhile, if you're dark-skinned, you can never get enough rays in North America. College, it turns out, is neither good nor bad—if you're not poor, what really matters is gaining admission, regardless of whether you go or not.

Given such complex and contradictory messages, perhaps it's time to scrap the parenting advice book and learn how to figure out things for ourselves. After all, since we have no common culture or history, we American parents are constantly improvising on our kids whether we admit it or not. What this book argues is that we should rationalize these jazz-like parenting approaches into a scientific methodology: experimental parenting. *Parentology*—as I'm calling this approach—is all about trial and error, hypothesis and revision. For there's simply no one-formula-fits-all to raising successful, compassionate kids in today's impossibly complex and radically overstimulating world.

And just to be clear: by experiment, I don't mean raise one child in a box and one in the forest and see how they turn out. That is, experimental parenting doesn't mean randomly and injudiciously trying out any crackpot theory that springs to mind on your precious little guinea pigs. Parentology, in fact, involves first and foremost reading and deciphering the scientific literature— typically not referenced directly in a parenting book—drawing your own conclusions, and applying them to your kids. There is no counterfactual or control group for your kids, so keep good notes in your own lab manual.

I've discovered after my long professional journey as a scientist and my own personal journey that what really matters in the end is parental love as expressed through engagement. As one psychotherapist friend reports, "Nobody lies on my couch and complains that they got too *much* attention." My particular form of engagement—through the science of children—happens to fit both my skill set and what kind of kids I'd like to produce: independent, critical thinkers. But be careful what you wish for: I created creatures who question every aspect of my parenting and demand evidence for anything I request them to do.

What's more, over the course of my parental experience—one that included weeks in the neonatal intensive care unit with our firstborn, medicating our second child, and parental divorce—I eventually realized the limits of my professional calling: In the face of the unexpected challenges that each unique child brings, scientific objectivity is no match for the torrent of parental affection and protectiveness that I could not have anticipated feeling and which almost every parent recognizes.

That is, rather than try to tap into parental guilt and worry through providing a hard-to-follow formula (like three hours of violin practice a day), I aim to assuage those same feelings by telling parents that there are many roads to Carnegie Hall. And, more important, most roads to a happy, decent, caring, well-adjusted, independent adult don't necessarily lead through Carnegie Hall or MIT. So, instead of a rigid formula, focused on a single, societal-identified definition of success, I offer an insurgency strategy: more flexibility and fluidity, attention to (often counterintuitive, myth-busting) research, but adaptation to each child's unique and changing circumstances. Trial and error. Hypothesis revision and more experimentation about what works. In other words, the scientific method.

Kids won't break—mine haven't (so far, at least). Most parents fret that they are deviating from some ideal norm—that they are somehow weird and this eccentricity will get in the way of their kids' opportunities. I can't imagine you'll think that after you read about my family and parenting practices. And if the science of children seems intimidating, don't worry; it seemed daunting to me at first, too, and I'm a professional social scientist.

In fact, despite my PhD, my future wife and I blundered into our first pregnancy about as unscientifically as could be imagined. For starters, we hardly knew each other at the time we conceived. We had been going out less than six months by the night of my June birthday when the seed of our daughter E was planted. We weren't married. Natalie had just lost her health insurance—not to mention her right to stay in the country on a student visa—on account of having left Stanford. You could say that E was an accident, but that would be like saying crashing into the freeway median after purposely closing your eyes at seventy-five miles per hour was a mistake. We weren't some naïfs in the Victorian era. We were folks with advanced degrees who knew full well how babies were made. We were just caught up in the thrall of sexual possibility and thus went about our proverbial business without any protection or long-term plan.

So while we weren't quite *Sixteen and Pregnant*, I really didn't know what I was getting myself into. I had literally never held an infant in my arms. If you adjust for my education level and the fact that we lived in San Francisco and then Manhattan, I was practically a teen parent. (I was twenty-eight—Natalie was thirty-one, when E was born.) As the second eldest of ten, Natalie, by contrast, had much experience with raising children. She had, in fact, pinched off her sister's umbilical cord in the backseat of the car on the way to the hospital back in her native Australia. Little Coralie, number nine, had been born in the parking lot of a church where they had just dropped off the eldest son for choir practice. And Natalie, herself, had borne a daughter, Jamba—now twenty-six years old—a decade before we ever met.

While that pregnancy had gone smoothly, ours certainly did not. One day during her first trimester, Natalie bled profusely in the shower. Chunks of tissue followed. We scooped up the tissue from the drain and rushed it to the UCSF obstetrics group practice. They poked it around under the microscope and declared that, luckily, there was no fetal matter in it. Then they sent us home with no instructions. Evidently, medical professionals view the first trimester through a Darwinist lens: If you lose a baby before week 12 or 13, they assume it had something major wrong with it and that it wasn't really viable. It's nature's do-over; but of course, that doesn't comfort those would-be parents who have endured a miscarriage. Nor did it assuage our own anxieties.

The bleeding returned when Natalie was on another business trip back to San Francisco. While in California, she also experienced what she thought were harmless Braxton-Hicks contractions. She checked into UCSF Medical Center again. There they strapped a fetal heart rate monitor across her belly and a blood pressure cuff onto her arm. They kept her there for a few hours, and then, since the fetal heart rate had been normal the whole time, released her again without specific instructions. Before leaving, she asked if it would be all right to fly given the contractions she was feeling. They told her it would be—even though bleeding in the third trimester is an entirely different story and should be dealt with seriously, we later discovered.

We had put a down payment on a small apartment in New York, where we had moved in anticipation of commuting to New Haven to teach at Yale, but we were having trouble getting a mortgage. As a result of the delay in closing on the unit, we camped out in a little storage room that was in a building attached to my parents' apartment. I had purchased a dorm-sized fridge, a hotplate, and a microwave oven. While it was December and snowy outside, the storage room was overheated by steam pipes that left the air totally arid. On one of the nights not too long after spotting in California, Natalie nudged me awake. "Dalton," she rustled me, before doubling over in pain. "Dalton, I'm getting contractions."

I mumbled something and rolled over, trying to ignore the early morning pressure in my bladder. "Dalton," she repeated, "we need to go to the hospital."

The word "hospital" tripped my attention wires. I jumped up and slipped on some jeans. The cold air of January 1, 1998, blasted us in the face when I finally forced the door open against the Hudson River wind that kept it shut, as if it knew that people shouldn't be out and about at five in the morning in the dead of winter. There was not a taxi in sight.

We pushed ahead another block eastward toward St. Vincent's Hospital. Still no cab. It was only four blocks in total, and we ended up walking the whole way. We had planned to take a natural child birthing class. We had planned to have a place to live by March 5, Natalie's due date. Other than folic acid to prevent spina bifida, we hadn't even gotten around to researching which dietary supplements Natalie should be taking. We knew that tuna was controversial—good for the DHA and EPA long-chain fatty acids that were meant to aid fetal brain development, but bad due to the risk of mercury in large fish. Given that the pregnancy was unplanned, all Natalie had done by way of preparations was quit drinking and smoking the moment the white dipstick came back with the "positive" double stripe.

They rushed us in, past the crashing speed freaks, past a couple of people who had no visible ailments, past even the older black man who was groaning, all the while holding a blood soaked towel wrapped around his left hand. Maybe it was our white skin, maybe it was our insurance card, or perhaps mothers and unborn children come before all else, but my own childhood experiences of waiting for hours in urban emergency rooms after this or that playground accident were washed away as they held open the double-swinging doors and guided Natalie to a waiting wheelchair. Soon, we were in the maternity ward, Natalie's stomach strapped with a sensor-adorned belt that looked like it might have formed part of one of her interactive techno-art pieces, her ankles gripped by blood pressure cuffs that inflated and deflated of their own accord to keep her circulation flowing through her lower extremities. The stomach belt was attached to a heart rate monitor that beeped with each pump of our little girl's heart.

A resident came into the room and introduced herself. She was Russian or from one of the other republics that once made up the Soviet Union. She told us that the good news was the baby was fine, that her heart rate appeared normal, and she didn't seem to be in "fetal distress." She told us that she would like our permission to give Natalie a shot of betamethasone, a steroid that was not for Natalie herself, but rather was intended for the baby, to mature her lungs more rapidly. The leading cause of infant mortality among premature babies, she announced, was respiratory failure due to a lack of surfactant—that is, mucus—in the lungs. It is the wet surfactant that allows for the exchange of carbon dioxide for oxygen. Before we could even answer, the doctor added that she also wanted to give Natalie an IV containing magnesium sulfate, to slow—and hopefully stop—the contractions.

Through her pain, Natalie piped up, "What are the long-term consequences of these treatments for children?"

"We know," the doctor answered, "the longer baby stays inside, the better. We don't know of problems with magnesium sulfate." Her English was quite broken with the exception of the names of the chemical compounds, which she seemed to pronounce without even the slightest accent.

I could see the organic, drug-resistant Natalie coming into focus, regaining control of the body she now shared with our daughter. The tension in the room was rising, and I feared that Natalie would explode at this poor foreign medical graduate. Instead, she consciously exhaled as another contraction kicked in. When it finally released its grip on her womb, she turned to me: "Do a search on the long-term effects. Except that they never study long-term effects. Medical research is so ridiculously myopic."

"There is no time for research," the ob/gyn said.

I looked at Natalie; she nodded to me, confirming her orders, so I ignored the doctor and ran with my laptop to find a connection to the internet. When I had downloaded all the abstracts I could find on the PubMed database, I sprinted back to her bedside, each loping step leading me down the path of what would be a long apprenticeship as a Parentologist. "You were right, of course," I read, in staccato, between my short breaths. "There are no long-term follow-up studies on the short term use of steroids in utero or on the magnesium sulfate."[1]

With the steroid injection, we would be getting an insurance policy on her breathing (but perhaps an insurance policy we didn't actually need, given that she was at 32 weeks gestation, not 26), but what price would we pay in the end? Would she be more anxious as an adult? Shorter? Would she be more prone to heart disease or stroke? There were literally no answers on these questions—certainly with respect to humans where doing double-blind trials was out of the question—but not even in mouse models, at least as far as I could determine as I sat at the hospital bedside and scrolled through the studies I had downloaded. Back then, I didn't know about the hypothalamus-pituitary-adrenal (HPA) axis and the long-term effects of stress hormones in utero in mouse studies. And they weren't in the human-centric Medline/PubMed databases I searched at the time.

I could see from Natalie's face that her dreams of natural childbirth were crumbling with each tick of the fetal heart monitor.

"Okay, then?" The doctor asked. I think the fact that she was a woman and of the same ethnic stock as the ancestrally Ukrainian Natalie reassured her. At least it wasn't a pompous, male American doctor who talked down to us. She inserted a syringe into the port attached to Natalie's IV and pressed down on the plunger. Our daughter's fate was thus altered by medical science.

As it turns out, I later learned that mice that were stressed in utero developed a different kind of biological response to stress later in life than those who enjoyed a Zen gestation. All of us get a spike in cortisol (the natural equivalent of cortisone) when a lion (or our boss) roars at us. The signal of danger travels down our hypothalamus to the anterior pituitary gland which, in turn, releases a penultimate hormone that stimulates our adrenal glands to pump the stress hormone into our system—getting our blood pumping to our brain and muscles so that we can sprint away from our boss or rear up on our hind quarters as we tell her to "take this job and shove it"—in the immortal words of Johnny Paycheck. Of course, this heightened state of mental awareness and physical prowess diverts metabolic energy away from the everyday business of being alive. We stop digesting whatever is in our gut as blood flows to our extremities. Other organ systems are likewise neglected. We don't spend many resources on growing our bones, for example, since we don't know if we are going to survive today, let alone ask someone to the prom senior year.

Hence, kids stressed in childhood or in utero tend to be stunted in stature.

Since cortisol and other steroids have a pretty destructive effect on our bodies (something that always haunts me when I think back to the betamethasone that E received), we want to shut down the acute stress response as quickly as possible once we have scared away the mugger with our arched back and fanned-out tail feathers. Luckily, there's a negative feedback loop built into the system: Our hypothalamus has glucocorticoid receptors that shut down the whole system when cortisol binds to them. But here's the catch: Folks who experience continually high levels of stress in the womb or during their childhood tend to shut down production of those receptors—that is, they end up with fewer of them. Since they have fewer off-switches, it takes longer for their cortisol levels to diminish to non-emergency levels. So, those who have experienced a childhood of having to be constantly vigilant due to a dangerous neighborhood, a conflict-ridden household, or a parent who herself was stressed while pregnant maintain elevated cortisol for much longer, taking a toll on their systems. This toll is exacted on the organ systems whose maintenance is neglected during the stress response. Also, the stress response promotes inflammation to protect against bacteria—presumably from open wounds we may suffer—while ratcheting down our protection against viruses. Unfortunately, in the developed world viruses are generally a larger threat and repeated inflammation can lead to chronic disease ranging from arthritis to coronary heart disease.

Finally, cortisol is a prime suspect to explain why poor folks suffer from higher rates of metabolic disorders such as type 2 (late-onset) diabetes and high blood pressure. This latter dynamic may, in part, stem from the fact that we don't do what we used to do when we were stressed: run and fight. Since the stress response elevates our blood pressure, sends energy to our muscles, and generally makes us ready to partake in some serious physical activity, it also tells us to eat afterward. The only problem is that in our modern society, we most likely have not spent a lot of extra calories during our period of stress so we don't need to eat as much as our body is telling us. Result: gain in fat.

In fact, a differential stress response is one of the important ways that poverty and racism lead to different health outcomes—since being at the bottom of a power hierarchy tends to lead to a more prolonged stress response.[2] And, in turn, the mice with a prolonged stress response tended to do worse on cognitive tests.[3] Unless, critically, the environment in which the test is administered is also stressful—then the mice who were stressed out early in life do better since they are naturally attuned to such conditions and thus better able to deal with them.

As it turns out, a brilliant researcher decided to push the logic on the stressed mice. Indeed the mice that were reared in the murine retreat equivalent of Esalen did better on their rodent SATs when the tests were administered in a calm classroom. However, when the exams were themselves given under stressful conditions (like with a cat scratching at the glass, electric shocks, or whatever other horrors lab technicians thought up) it was the ghetto mice

who outperformed their laid-back counterparts. Like modera-
tion itself, even stress can be beneficial if absorbed in small doses.
Score one for Mother Nature: Evolution is no dope—mice pups
and human rug rats are neurologically programmed to best suit
the environment that awaits them. Problems arise when there is
a mismatch between their early experiences and the challenges of
later life.

A Chinese neonatologist slipped into the room with a mobile
sonogram unit on wheels. "Let's take a look at this baby, yes?"
he asked in an upward lilting tone that fit his accent. "May I?"
he asked, before lifting Natalie's gown to expose her not-swollen-
enough belly. She had been rehearsing with a dance troupe of
pregnant women, practicing for a performance two weeks hence
of the "Expectant Tango" in an alternative theater space on the
now bohemian Lower East Side of Manhattan. She had missed
many rehearsals what with her trip to San Francisco and other
distractions, but Natalie was physically deft and could make up
for lack of practice with spontaneous agility and ability—even
among a group of formerly professional dancers. They were all
due around the same time in early March—this was key to the
choreography—but the one time I picked her up from rehearsal,
I had noticed that Natalie's stomach protruded much less than
those of the other women, who were equally slight in frame.
Now, as the neonatologist lubed up her stomach with jelly
to ensure good contact, I worried that the baby was not only
premature, but also small for her gestational age—in double
jeopardy.

"Let's see now," he announced as he fired up the machine and touched the white handle that looked like an electric massager to the spot where her uterus would be. "Look at that."

Suddenly, the image of a baby curled on the screen in white on black. It was a real human child. It had been about two and a half months since we had last seen her at the twenty-week mark. Now she appeared as a real infant, sucking her thumb, and not merely the fishbone that she had looked like before.

"I just need to take some measurements," he said, pushing buttons to mark Xs on the screen where her long bones started and ended. Then he noted her head diameter and estimated her total length, had she been stretched out. When it was all done, he announced, "Looks like she's four and a half pounds or so."

Natalie and I squeezed hands and let the air out of our lungs in synchronicity. We had been told that she would probably be in the two- to three-pound range given the timing. This was an enormous relief, considering. "Plus or minus a half pound error," he added. I immediately added the half pound in my head to make her five even. I could tell by Natalie's face she subtracted it with worry. "Very important to keep her inside as long as you can," he sighed. "Each week is ten more points of IQ."

A spark of rage landed on my sleeve. An urge to grab the doctor's head and bash it against the sharp corner of the sonogram machine seized hold of me. I wanted to smash his head one time for every IQ point. How dare he say something like that? Natalie must have sensed my impulse. When the doctor left the room, she took my hand again and said, "Our daughter is going to be smart, beautiful, charming, independent, healthy," she began to peter out, so I jumped in.

"Loving, happy . . ."

"Balanced, friendly . . ."

"Strong."

"Sensitive."

"And infinitely wonderful."

I stroked the tears from her eyes, and she did the same for me. This litany of traits became a refrain for us those next weeks in the hospital and for years to come after that as well.

A few days later—not nearly long enough—E made her way into the world. The next two months in the neonatal intensive care unit were filled with the numbness of crisis management. E was still a stranger to me. I wasn't the sort to fall in love right away. I had to get to know her first. But that didn't lessen the intensity of my sleepless apprehension. It was as if Natalie and I had arrived at the scene of a car accident. It didn't matter if the person pinned behind the steering wheel was friend or foe; once you pulled over, you had committed yourself to the Samaritan course of action. It wouldn't be until E had transformed from a medical crisis into a real gurgling, crawling person reaching developmental milestones that I would be truly-madly-deeply taken with her.

After she got out of the hospital, E spent most of the rest of her first year of life on a heart monitor since she experienced brachycardia (sudden, dramatic drops in her heart rate due to errant parasympathetic vagal nerve signals that told the body to slow down). She was developmentally delayed; didn't speak till well after two years of age; and had to undergo eye surgery and several years of patching one of her eyes thanks to the fact that her eyes were not synced to each other and that one had fallen behind in visual acuity so needed to be retrained. E also suffered from sensory integration disorder, which is a stimulus processing issue—that is, she had challenges in sorting through various stimuli coming into her brain to prioritize her attention. Thus she often got distracted by what she was doing and was unresponsive to outside stimuli; she also had trouble dealing with change. To this day, she gets mad whenever anyone in the family gets a haircut. To boot, she was muscularly hypertonic—which basically means that she was always tense to compensate for weak trunk strength. E received early intervention services to try to address all these complications and was enrolled in special education when it came time for grade school.

In an ironic twist, shortly before she had been born, I had started on my second big research project: the effect of birth weight on life outcomes. I compared siblings from a study of 5,000 U.S. households who differed on their birth weight. I found that those who were heavier—i.e. of normal birth weight, greater than five pounds eight ounces (2,500 grams)—were about 50 percent more likely than their low birth weight brothers or sisters to graduate from high school in a timely fashion (i.e. when they are supposed to, as opposed to getting a GED or other equivalency degree later on). Timely completion of secondary school, in turn, is the best predictor of going on to and completing a four-year college degree. That 50 percent effect was huge. It was more disadvantageous, it turns out, to be low birth weight than to be black in America.[4]

Natalie, it goes without saying, banned the book that emerged from my birth weight research from our house.

"For god's sake," my sister, in turn, pleaded with me in case life continued to imitate research, "can't you study something like lottery winnings?"

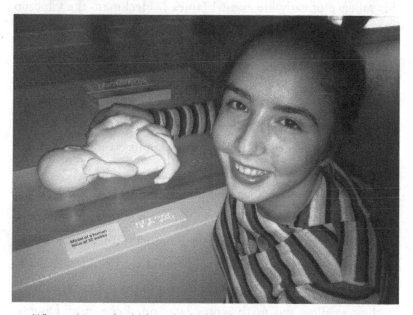

What a 32-week-old fetus looks like then and thirteen years later.

Little did I know, my birth weight study was part of a growing social movement led by no less than then first lady Hillary Clinton and her friend from the Children's Defense Fund, Marian Wright Edelman. After the Clinton health-care disaster, Hillary devoted herself to cookie bakeoffs and children's issues—penning *It Takes a Village* in the process. The book's focus on the importance of early childhood conditions was ahead of its time, since it really wasn't until the 2000s that social scientists had started amassing evidence that environmental influences (i.e. nurture) early in life were the most consequential. The earlier the more important—all the way back to and including prebirth life. By the mid-2000s, the ultimate imprimatur had been placed on this salience of early life events: James J. Heckman, the Chicago Nobel economist, reanalyzed data from a preschool pilot study in Ypsilanti, Michigan, that had formed the basis of the Head Start program and found major effects. He wrote a series of papers on early skill formation with scintillating titles such as "Estimating the Technology of Cognitive and Noncognitive Skill Formation," which appeared in the most prestigious economics journal, *Econometrica*, in 2010.

In recent years, this scientific literature on prenatal effects has blossomed into other areas like radiation exposure and maternal stress. For example, my colleague Florencia Torche studied an earthquake in her native Chile and found that children born to those pregnant mothers who were closest to the epicenter suffered in their reading and math scores later on. Economist Douglas Almond and his colleagues found that kids in utero in Sweden in 1987 were adversely affected all the way through high school (and perhaps beyond) by the Chernobyl nuclear disaster if their mothers lived in a province over which the radioactive cloud rained its iodine-131. This, despite the fact that the levels of radioactivity

were well below the IAEA safety guidelines. Other economists—
Bashir Muzumder and his coauthors—found that daytime fasting
during Ramadan by pregnant mothers hurt the IQs of kids in
utero.[5] And 9/11 caused more spontaneous abortions of boys and
probably hurt the kids who were in utero at the time. The list goes
on. (And you thought that just limiting yourself to one glass of red
wine and quitting cigarettes was enough . . .)

I hope you had more scientific foresight than we did. If so, you
would have had your kids in autumn of a year when few other
parents were having kids. Kids from small birth cohorts tend
to enjoy more opportunities in life since there tend to be more
job and housing vacancies available to them.[6] Meanwhile, in the
Northern Hemisphere, kids born in the spring are the worst off
in terms of life expectancy and a host of other outcomes; kids
born in the fall do the best. Researchers are still trying to figure
out why there is a seasonal effect. It does not appear to be simply
a class difference in who is having kids when. It is possibly due
to viral loads experienced by babies and mothers at different
points in the year: kids born in the winter months are exposed to
a heavier germ burden that may weaken their bodies for decades
to come. More likely, this seasonal pattern of life expectancy is
due to the availability of food: Kids who are born during the fall
harvest do the best, and those born after the winter, by which
time food would be running out, are historically at greatest risk.
What's amazing is that it is not just greatest risk of dying as an
infant, but risk of death once they've already survived to age 50.
Boy, that's one long shadow.[7]

Well if your kids were born during spring of a baby boom year, don't give up yet. They still have a chance to succeed in life. Or at least that's what I told myself. And I am not speaking from any hippy-dippy perspective where all I want for them is to be quote-unquote "happy." I have devoted my career to studying traditional measures of socioeconomic success, after all; and if there's one thing I know, it's that all social scientists—and perhaps all academics—are studying themselves and their own unconscious obsessions. I have long been obsessed with societal "merit badges" so to speak—little markers that I was on the right path to please my elders. And my hopes for my kids were no different. I wanted what most middle-class parents desire for their offspring but are loath to admit these days—academic, career, and family success.

But now my life's work was going to be tested. No longer were my research studies abstract inquiries into the nature of economic opportunity in modern society. They were applicable to the very flesh and blood I cared about more than anything else in the world. Or, at least, I thought they were applicable. Soon I would learn firsthand how hard it was to rappel down the walls of the ivory tower and land safely in the kindergarten classroom. The first decision we faced when E came home from the hospital after five weeks in an incubator was whether or not to set up a crib for her or to receive her in our bed. With a public relations campaign against SIDS and a heart monitor attached to her, there was lots of social pressure to set up a bassinet for her. My friends asked how I'd ever expect a sex life again if we always had a baby in our bed. I countered that the Inuit all lived in one igloo and managed to reproduce just fine. Even my mother freaked out, worrying that we'd roll over and crush the poor little girl if we slept with her. She whipped out her original copy of Dr. Spock and pointed to the page where he advocated separate sleeping arrangements for infant and parents.[8]

But we felt like we had been deprived of our sweet baby for so long, always having had to scrub down with Betadine and put on hospital gowns before we could touch her in the hospital, so all we wanted to do was snuggle her at home. Instead of assembling a crib from IKEA, we ignored public opinion and blew up an air mattress and collapsed on the floor all together.

Luckily, we had a significant body of science on our side. Not to mention history. Young infants throughout human (and primate) history have tended to spend most of their time clinging to their caregiver, awake and asleep. This physical bonding, in turn, is important to the development of what psychologist John Bowlby called "secure attachment," in which the caregiver is highly responsive to the infant's needs.

To test children's attachments, Mary Ainsworth developed an experimental methodology called the "strange situation protocol." The primary caregiver would bring a one-year-old to a new room filled with novel toys. The securely attached kid would typically leave the parent to explore the toys, returning periodically to check in, perhaps showing off one of the items to Mom (or Dad or Grandma or Nanny, as the case may be). And then when the guardian left the room (on orders from the experimenter), the kid would soon notice and start crying. This secure kid, however, would eventually be soothed by another adult. When the parent returned, the child would greet her with relief and smiles in a big, heartfelt reunion.

Insecure attachments, which may result from neglect, abuse, or variable reinforcement from a parental unit, play out very differently in the "strange situation." Like Tolstoy's famous dictum about all unhappy families being unhappy in their own, unique way, insecure attachments come in a variety of flavors. One type—"ambivalent" or "resistant" attachment—results from variable responses from the parent to the child's needs over the course of infancy. This kid is very hesitant to leave the parent at all and is inconsolable when she leaves the room, but then reluctant to rebond upon her return. A second type of insecurely attached kid at first appears to be the most secure. This "avoidant" kid immediately engages with the toys upon entering the room, rarely checks back in with the parent, interacts just as well with a stranger, and is hardly bothered by parental absence—i.e. avoids intimacy with the parent. In our independence-obsessed culture, this kid was at first lionized by many as the best adapted. However, then some researchers had the brilliant notion of hooking these little tykes up to wires to measure their heart rate, respiration, and perspiration. What they found was that while they were indeed quiet and apparently calm on the outside, on the inside, they were the most anxious of all. Their wee hearts were racing. Ainsworth's colleague Mary Main also discovered a third form of insecure attachment she called "disorganized," which often resulted from parental abuse or trauma. These kids would often freeze up or rock themselves and approached their parents in strange ways (like walking backward toward them). Needless to say, the kids with any form of insecure attachment had more social difficulties with peers later on—especially in the context of intimate relationships. The goal, in essence, is not to have a baby who quiets herself down so the parents can get laid. It's to have a well-adjusted adult in twenty years. We were going to just keep cuddling E on our air mattress, lowering her cortisol levels, no matter what anyone else said, even if it was Dr. Spock.

2

Tying the Knot
(and I Don't Mean Marriage—
or the Umbilicus)

I'D LIKE to say that the experience with E taught me a lesson: to be more scientific in the way I approached my reproductive life. I'd like to say that, but I'd be lying if I did. Indeed, the hasty bedside literature review conducted in St. Vincent's Hospital was merely the first step in my transformation into a Parentologist. Faster than I could search the academic literature on premature babies, we were pregnant again. And yet, again, life imitated research.

Along with parental education, wealth, and pregnancy conditions, one of the strongest predictors associated with academic and monetary success is family size, or more precisely, the number of siblings. The consensus for decades has been that kids from smaller families excelled as compared to kids from larger families. Forget the mythology that only children are maladapted; they leave us in the dust. Some scholars even attribute a modest part of China's recent economic tear to the dividends of its one child policy (though that may eventually backfire when a small working-age population has to support a larger retiree class).

So, besides when they are born, how many siblings children have is one of the few other variables we can control. The problem for a long time was that we scientists were not 100 percent sure that the effect was real. There were lots of good theories to support it, of course, and it makes sense that with fewer kids in a house, each kid gets more parental resources. Furthermore, the intellectual climate (i.e. the level of dialogue at the dinner table, sense of order, and so on) of a household with two parents and one child where the average age is, say, 25, is a lot more elevated than the chaos of a household with two parents and four kids (where the average age might be under 15).

But there was always the nagging possibility that the entire statistical relationship between large families and poor academic performance was just the product of the fundamental differences between small and large families. Parents who have lots of kids tend to be of lower socioeconomic status, have lower IQs, tend to be more religious, and may not know how to use birth control effectively (like Natalie and I, clearly).[1]

Since I couldn't randomly sterilize some parents and force

others to mate repeatedly, in my research I was looking for a natural experiment to address this possibility. As it turns out, parents whose first two kids are of the same sex are more likely to go on to have additional kids (in search of the missing gender, of course) than parents whose first two are of opposite sex. It makes no difference if those same-sex kids are boys or girls, as it turns out (unless you are an Asian immigrant, in which case, there is heavy boy preference among the population). And whether you get same sex or opposite sex kids for your initial kids is random—like the coin toss in a double-blind experiment—so it's unrelated to parental IQ, religiosity, income, or anything else that might mess up our inference. Thus, in our research study, I compared parents who had same sex kids for their first two with those who had opposite sex kids for their first pair. I found that, indeed, those with same sex kids were significantly more likely to go on to have more kids, and when they did, I found that there was a cost to the additional children in terms of parental educational investment and student academic performance. But those costs were disproportionately borne by the (now) middle child (i.e. the second born). My study (done with Rebecca Glauber) is hardly the last word on the matter (there is never a last word in the science of children), but it does suggest that there may be detrimental effects of having additional kids on your existing ones—at least if you don't stop at two. You will have less time and money to invest in them, and the middle born(s) are going to be more likely to fall behind in school and be held back a grade.

That is, my research had shown that there was no birth order effect on success in families of two kids. But once you went to three or more, disadvantage for the middle one(s) emerged. It felt like stopping our carefree approach to reproduction was critical to E's and our new son Yo's future opportunities. We had already done enough damage by having them only eighteen months apart—while we were still dealing with E's catch-up growth and development. In addition to how many kids a family has, how closely they are spaced has also been shown to matter to their ultimate socioeconomic success: the closer the births are spaced, the more strain on the parents, and the worse the kids do educationally and economically later in life.[2]

Having come from such a pronatalist family of ten kids, Natalie would have kept popping them out fast and furious as long as she was physically able to, so any limitations to our mutual fertility fell squarely on my shoulders—or rather, on my testicles. There was no way I got married so that I could continue using condoms, and she refused to take the pill, so I was left with only one option: tying the knot. The vas deferens knot, that is. Not really tie, more like snip, actually.

But like the good Parentologist that I was now becoming out of necessity, I first checked the research on vasectomies. It turned out that men with vasectomies evinced a higher rate of prostate cancer. I postponed my appointment with the urologist so that I could dig a little deeper into the literature. What I found was that though there was that higher incidence of prostate cancer among the snipped, there was actually a lower death rate from prostate cancer. This was terribly good news. What it meant to me was that the higher diagnosis rate was probably just due to the fact that men who were forward-thinking, vigilant, or just plain neurotic enough (like me) to get a vasectomy were also probably more likely to go in for prostate tests, or that dudes with intact plumbing were being killed off before developing cancer by other things (like fast cars, booze, and dangerously tight rubbers). Meanwhile, the lower death rate for sterilized men probably stems from the fact that we are more likely to be hypochondriacs and are more likely to detect the cancer earlier (and thus cure it).

There was still one other loose end I had to tie up before scheduling the surgery: I needed to ejaculate into a cup. That is, I wanted to store sperm just in case I changed my mind in the future, once I forgot how overwhelmingly stinky diapers are. So I found a cryogenic laboratory in the Empire State Building. (I wanted a facility in the biggest phallic symbol I could find.) After I had abstained a few days from sex (which was easily accomplished given a postpartum, nursing wife) and from the sin of Onan (much harder) in order to store up the most sperm I could deliver in a single payload, I signed the paperwork that guaranteed my sperm's integrity and safety EXCEPT in cases of acts of God or terrorism and headed off to the room with the porno magazines. (Hence my concern on 9/11 that the Empire State building would be the terrorists' next target.)

When this was taken care of, I called back Dr. Wu and we met for the preoperative consultation. I explained the reasons for my delay and why I could now rest easy. But I did have one more question: "What percent of reversal operations are successful?" He didn't answer, so I thought he hadn't understood. "You know, reconnecting the plumbing."

"Now, you are sure you want to do this?" he asked me. "If you are freezing sperm and asking about reversals, you're probably not ready."

Clearly he either didn't understand economics and marketing or else already had his second home, sailboat, and Mercedes because he seemed to be talking me out of a lucrative procedure. "Do *you* not want to do this?" I turned the tables. I would have quoted Donald Rumsfeld on "known knowns," "known unknowns," and "unknown unknowns" as to why it's always better to keep all options open and recognize the limits of one's own foresight. But I couldn't since this was 2000, and he was not yet secretary of defense and thus hadn't yet uttered that memorable line to justify his botched handling of post-Saddam Iraq (a line, by the way, for which he received considerable ridicule even though it was logically consistent and even elegant). So instead, I just repeated my request: "What's the percentage, please?"

"Seventy-five."

"That's good enough for me." Based on my research, I figured my reserve troops in the Empire State Building gave me a 50 percent shot at future reproduction should I so desire it, and added to the 75 percent from rerouting the plumbing, I had a 125 percent success rate—better than before! (Just kidding, that's not how you add independent percentages. I was looking at an 87.5

percent chance of successfully knocking someone up if I changed my mind once I was done with this round of diapers.) The next day, a nurse shaved my balls and then Dr. Wu slit them open to make me 12.5 percent sterile. And my two kids' future test scores silently rose a notch or two.

3

But Maybe You *Should* Name Your Boy Sue: What's Not in a Name

UNLIKE HAVING fewer kids, birthing them in the Northern Hemisphere during October of a year when not many others are having kids, avoiding the mercury in fish (while still getting enough omega-3 and omega-9 fatty acids), and being rich, well-educated, and handsome to boot, there is *one thing* you can bequeath your kids that is entirely within your control.[1] I'm talking about selecting their names. We may not control what race or gender we bequeath our offspring (unless, of course, we are utilizing a sperm bank in the Empire State Building for IVF), but we do have say over their names. If you play it safe with Bill or Lisa, it probably means your kids will be marginally more likely to avoid risk, too. If you're like us and name them E or Yo, they are likely to grow up into weirdoes like their parents—or at least not work in middle management.

Early studies on names claimed that folks with strange ones were overrepresented in prisons and mental hospitals. But the more recent (and in my professional opinion, better) research actually comes to the opposite conclusion: Having a weird name makes you more likely to have impulse control since you get lots of practice biting your tongue when bigger, stronger, older kids make fun of you in the schoolyard. This study makes me happy, given the growing scientific literature around the extreme importance of impulse control and its close cousin, delayed gratification. These two, some argue, are even more important than raw IQ in predicting socioeconomic success, marital stability, and even staying out of prison.

It all started with the "marshmallow test," Walter Mischel's experiment where he presented four-year-old kids with a marshmallow and then told them that if they refrained from eating it until the researcher returned, they'd get an extra one. [2]

The researchers found that when they instructed the children not to think about the marshmallow, they actually gave in faster. Evidently, it was kind of like telling someone not to think of a big pink elephant. (I'm guessing an image of a colorful pachyderm popped into your mind just then.) The kids who lasted the longest were the ones told to think about the physical characteristics of the marshmallow: its texture, its shape and color, its smell. When they confronted and isolated it as an object with separable qualities, they were able to master their desire for it, as it turned out. Such an approach has since been recommended for everything from dieting to battling premature ejaculation.

But there was a small minority of kids who ate the marshmallow right away no matter what strategies they were given to cope with the temptation. Evidently, these kids were doing life without parole when Mischel chased them down years later. What's more, the longer the kid could wait, the higher his or her SAT score. Once the rest of the social science world got hold of these results, an intellectual feeding frenzy ensued around the issue of such "noncognitive skills."[3]

So the idea of endowing my children with names that would force them to bite their tongues and thereby raise their noncognitive IQs was appealing to me. What's more, I can personally attest to this effect of weird names since everyone called me "Dolphin" growing up, and there was not a single thing I could do about it, given that I was a skinny little nerd.

And besides, what's a fairly unique name in one decade could become commonplace later on; imagine my shock when I read a few years ago that "Dalton" had made it into the top twenty-five list of boys names; or my horror when I learned that not only are there now a bunch of five-year-old Daltons running around town, I am also no longer the only Dalton Conley in the world. This eighteen-year-old Michigan-punk Dalton Conley, daltonconley@gmail.com, added insult to injury by staking his Gmail claim before I could. This other Dalton Conley has so much attachment to his Google account that he refused to even entertain my crass offers to buy the address off him. Moreover, he hasn't done me the courtesy of forwarding misdirected mail or letting the authors of such email know that they've reached the wrong person. Or perhaps he just registered the account and then forgot all about it. So, I suppose the worst case scenario is getting teased throughout childhood and then still ending up with a common name by the time you reach adulthood; though somehow I doubt that Yo will ever hit the top one hundred, let alone the top twenty-five.

Since naming is the subject of this chapter, I better go ahead and explain the origin of our kids' names. When E was born, we had hardly given a thought to her name—not only because she was born eight weeks early but also because Natalie superstitiously believes that to name an unborn child is to give it the evil eye. With all the confusion of the conditions surrounding her birth and our sleepless nights thereafter in the NICU, we had only gotten down to a short list of various names that started with E—including "Early" and "Etchbrook," the latter being the middle name my mother gave herself when she was a kid. (Normal names like Elizabeth were not on the list.) We also wanted a gender-neutral name. I had, in fact, suggested "Co," which was a feminist pronoun in the 1970s that was meant to be a third, gender-neutral personal pronoun to allow us to avoid the clunky "she or he." Needless to say, Co didn't catch on during the bra-burning era, nor did it in our household in 1998. So we agreed to disagree on our list of E- names and just left it at that, deciding that she could choose what it stood for when she was old enough.

We figured that she'd go through a long phase of thinking her parents too weird and ask to be referred to as Ellen (my mother's name), or Emily, or something else relatively common before reverting, in her twenties, to just plain E. So far, however, she's stuck with the family circus freaks and calls herself E, correcting everyone when they think she's saying, "Eve." Little did we know that we were channeling the zeitgeist and that within a year or two, we'd all be living in the E-age of eBay, E*TRADE, e-zines, e-commerce, and so on. Oh well. And if you say that's the weirdest name you've ever heard, you clearly don't read the *New York Times* carefully, since if you did, you'd quite frequently see the byline Jennifer 8. Lee (who, I might add, chose the number herself when she was a teenager, and she turned out okay, despite the sinking ship of print journalism).

When we announced our selection to my family, my sister visibly blanched. "Well, she can choose what it stands for, right?" Clearly, she was counting on the fact that kids rebel against their parents and that E would therefore turn out to be a normal Elizabeth having two freaks for progenitors. All I can say is that E was the first kid to write her name in her preschool (but obviously that got quite boring after a while). And she never had another kid in her class with the same name, unlike my sister's eldest son, who had to revert to Dante C. (Conley-Leonardi) so as not to be confused with the other Dante in kindergarten.

As for Yo—well, we had already let E choose her own name, so in the cause of creativity, we had to come up with some other schtick for her brother. The idea was to confound ethnic expectations when it came to names. So we thought about Spanish names, but the problem with that would be that folks would just assume he was a white dude from Spain. We considered some African American names, but when tried on a white kid, they just sounded like he was a slave owner or a white Muslim. That left us with Asian names. Why not reverse assimilate—naming a white kid, something East Asian to counterbalance all the Howard Chungs across America?

I, personally, preferred Yo-Xing. I liked that his initials would be YX, the chromosomes for a male. I also liked the visual aspect of Xing in that it also meant "crossing" as written in traffic signs: SLOW, CHILDREN X-ING. And how cool is it to have X as a middle initial? It worked in a subtle nod to black power and deference to the Asian ethnic community all in one. And that's not all: Yo was both "I" as in "myself" in Spanish and "You" or "Hey" in New York street slang. But I made a mistake. I was so excited that I couldn't stop myself from blabbing the name nomination before the kid had made his way out into the blinding light of the world. So it was no longer acceptable to the superstitious Natalie. She did, however, agree to Yo.

Since we (or at least I) were pretty sure that Yo would represent the end of our fertility train, we had to get all other tributes into his name. I had been really into Robert Graves's *I, Claudius* that summer as we awaited Yo's arrival to the world, and he was born in August, so his second name became Augustus after the Roman emperor. That pagan moniker was followed by a tribute to my mother's mother, Eisner (her maiden name), and my mother's father (his last name, Alexander). These family names were followed by Weiser, the last name of a recently deceased close colleague of Natalie's who hired her to work at Xerox PARC—the think tank from which Steve Jobs stole the mouse and the idea of the computer desktop full of icons.

Perhaps it was thanks to the fact that Yo had survived the susceptible period of infancy, but three years later Natalie agreed that Xing would be pretty cool to add to his name. And as long as I was legally changing his name anyway, we thought it only fair that he could choose a name to add—thereby giving him some of the interactivity we had offered his older sister by providing her only a first initial. So, little Yo came with me to the courthouse and inserted "Heyno"—we think he probably thought it was his name already because so many folks were calling "Hey! No!" to this wild little man, who, for example, decided a couple times to run out of our ground-floor apartment buck naked. He also added "Knuckles," another family name—but of my childhood canine. Why should dead humans be the only ones honored through the recycling of their names, anyway? We weren't species-ists, after all. At the registry, the clerk informed us that when the judge officially approved our request, Yo would have the longest name on record in New York City.

The *New York Times* decided to run a story on Yo, replete with a photo of the little rascal, and since broadcast news often chases stories that the *Times* runs, suddenly we were inundated with requests for media appearances.[4] Though I turned down most of them, I did agree to take the kids onto Anderson Cooper's CNN show. I pitched E as well—asking why not have the kid with the shortest name, too?—and made both their participations a condition of agreeing to Yo's appearance in my effort to be fair to my two offspring. It went relatively well, despite the fact that Yo bit me repeatedly during the five-minute interview and kicked his shoe off, almost hitting Cooper in the face. (He chomped down on me between the thumb and my index finger, and I was quite proud of myself for managing not to flinch on camera. The flying shoe was really my fault since, being a miser, I always bought them a size too big in order to reduce the number of new shoes I'd need to purchase over the course of their childhoods.) My rationale for subjecting the kids to this media invasion was, of

Important to demystify television for the young 'uns so they don't get addicted to the boob tube later in life. Note son masticating father.

course, that they needed to be prepared for any experience from homeless refugee on up to media superstar. Why not start young?

I guess I probably should have expected that certain folks would not appreciate our sense of playfulness when it came to names, but I certainly didn't anticipate the onslaught of internet condemnation. Now, if Yo ever googles himself, he's most likely to read about how his parents are child abusers for saddling him with such a burden in nomenclature and that his father was awarded the "Fucktard of the Decade" prize by one blogger (thank you very much).[5] Yo, himself, must have felt self-conscious about his weird name (even in the progressive enclave of downtown Manhattan): he decided during kindergarten that his name was Dragon (misspelled as Dragin) and that we should all refer to him as such. Then during another period of elementary school, it morphed into "Sean." Unlike his parent-pleasing firstborn sister, he was putting the interactivity into his name, hacking it back to normal whether we liked it or not. Even I had to admit that when I shouted his name across the playground or down the street, as in "Yo, come back here!" or "Hurry up, Yo!" I felt pretty self-conscious when everyone turned around thinking I was calling out to them. Ultimately, however, Yo reverted to Yo; for this we have to thank gangster rap. He was happy that he wouldn't have to change his name when he went professional with the hip-hop lyrics he was starting to pen:

> *Yo, my name is Yo;*
> *I come from New Haven, not Mexico.*[6]

I've got bad etiquette,
Because I was born in Connecticut . . .

Aside from launching Yo's hip-hop career, their names do not seem to be having any discernible effect on their lives . . . *yet*. E has the willpower of a Jedi master, which she had even before she realized that her name was anything out of the ordinary. Yo, meanwhile, is as impulsive as a cocaine-addicted lab rat. The name has not appeared to have any effect whatsoever on his ability to suppress urges. What I can definitively say is that their names have been their destiny in one way at least: Everyone knows them. Kids from grades that for middle schoolers are as far away as the Pleistocene—like eighth grade to their sixth or fifth—know exactly who they are. It wasn't Anderson Cooper. Nor was it Steven Levitt and Stephen Dubner including Yo (and his freakish parents) in their bestseller *Freakonomics*; it was just the wind of gossip rustling the grapevine of downtown New York. Other kids, and more to the point, their parents, were fascinated to meet the actual people behind the strange names. In a public school where the kids of the rich and famous were a dime a dozen, E and Yo enjoyed a fame that rivaled that of Sarah Jessica Parker's or Daniel Day-Lewis's kids. The challenge for them, then, wasn't to unball their fists or bite their tongues. It was to live up to a level of notoriety that preceded them and for which they had done nothing but be born.

4

The Best Thesaurus Is
a Human Thesaurus:
How to Read to Your Kids

WE NEED to talk about Yo's reading." My stomach dropped when she said this—as any parent's would. Never a good thing to hear from your child's first-grade teacher. (But, of course, a lot better than hearing it from his sixth-grade teacher.) He had scored below the 5th percentile in reading, she explained to us as we all perched on little chairs as if we were riding clown bicycles. I tried to stay focused on what she was saying, but my mind was wandering to psychometrics, as I wondered how they could even have enough measurement granularity in a first-grade reading assessment to break students into such a fine-grained rank order.

Instead of calling the teacher a jerk and blaming her for his reading deficit—as my initial, defensive, emotional response would have had me do—I rationalized that their assessment was bunk due to measurement error.

You really can't measure a four-year-old's intelligence, or reading ability, for that matter. Depending on whether I wanted them to get into special ed or the gifted program, I was able to drive my kids' test scores up and down at will by adjusting how much food and sleep they got before the exams. There is simply too much variability at that age to get anything more than a crude estimate of a kid being relatively "bright" or "dull." Yet we still rank-order kids from the age of two. The best anecdtoal evidence to show how measurement error declines with age comes from Hunter, the highly selective public school in New York City. There are only two entry points for Hunter: you can test and interview at age four for kindergarten admission, or you can apply to come in at seventh grade. Seventh-grade admission is based solely on an exam. Kindergarten entry is a more rigorous process. First you have to pass an IQ test. Then you have to go for an in-person interview. The kindergarten entrants get thirteen years of exposure to the great Hunter education, which boasts the supposedly highest-functioning peers in New York City. The seventh graders get six years. Guess which kids do better on their high school SATs and other such measures? The ones who went to Hunter for *less* time do best. Not only is this evidence that schools don't matter all that much, these results show that measurement error in picking "winners" at early ages is—to put it mildly—significant.

"We'd like him to come in for early morning tutoring three

days a week until he's up to grade level," the general education teacher explained while the special ed teacher nodded. We always placed our kids into special ed since the "integrated" class had two teachers to the regular ed's one—not to mention other aides. If there is one factor that matters in school—with randomized trials to back up the claim—it is low student-to-teacher ratios. So having more adult attention always trumped consideration about peer quality or stigma in our minds.

It was, of course, hard to resist a teacher's authoritative advice. I was anxious about potentially alienating the teachers—which I deemed the worst possible parental move given the power they have to shape your kid's self-perception, social life, and cognitive development between the hours of nine and three. (See chapter 9 for more on this.) So I bit my lip and didn't rattle off the research that showed that early reading—as measured by the ability to make sense of the squiggles on a page or screen—was only weakly correlated with later verbal ability. In fact, if you look across Europe, it's in the U.K. that kids read the earliest and in Finland where they read the latest.[1] When the kids are retested at age fourteen, the Brits do the worst and the Finns are at the top of the European rankings. So there.

In fact, adults who learned to read on their own—i.e. without explicit word decoding training—read faster and have a bigger vocabulary than those taught with phonics. Of course, this study was based on a matched sample of grown-ups, so it could be that the average performance of the "phonics kids" group was brought down by subjects who really *needed* phonics growing up, having been slow to learn to decode sentences on their own. While the reading wars will surely continue, there is at least some consensus emerging that 60-plus percent of kids will indeed learn to read just fine without any training in decoding. Since dyslexia didn't run in our families, I was going with the odds that my kids were among the majority who didn't need phonics.

What really matters in the long run, in my view, is reading comprehension. So I asked, "How did he score on the rest of the verbal assessment?"

They proceeded to sheepishly admit that Yo had scored eleventh grade on vocabulary (through an oral test, obviously, since the little dude couldn't read) and at a twelfth-grade level on reading comprehension (again, when being read aloud to). Not wanting to alienate the teachers, I suppressed the sly smile of a proud parent, which threatened to crack my countenance, and, in the end, I agreed to schlep him there three mornings a week. But mostly we were late and were locked out (school rules were that if you were more than ten minutes late for your early morning tutelage, you couldn't enter the building). And, as I had figured (or rather, hoped and prayed), the mechanics of word decoding eventually came to him.[2]

I really hadn't been so worried about his reading since all I did 24/7 was read to my kids. I read so many books to them, and they liked literature so much, that at least until they became adolescents, I could threaten them with no books or reading as punishment. I had never focused on the mechanics of reading—the word decoding that the Bush administration pushed so hard in its Early Reading First initiative that was part of the No Child Left Behind legislation. Not to say that I didn't *ever* have them sound out words, but I pretty much left that to the school to address. Luckily I happened to have had cutting-edge research on my side.

Right before E and Yo were born a report was published by psychologists Betty Hart and Todd Risley that has since been cited thousands of times. In the study, observers went to the homes of welfare families and those of middle-class families. They simply counted the number of words spoken aloud in the presence of young kids in the home. The difference was staggering. The middle-class moms were virtual Robin Williams chatterboxes. Extrapolating their observations over a putative four-year preschool window, they calculated that the middle-class kids heard 45 million words. The poor children, by contrast, were exposed to a mere 13 million bons mots. To make matters worse, this difference in words spoken seemed to explain the gap in cognitive achievement by the time the kids reached school age (which is, in turn, the root of most achievement differences played forward).

Confirming this research—albeit indirectly—were findings that came out of the "mommy wars." Namely, rather than it being good or bad per se for a mother to stay home with her young children, the effect seemed to depend on the socioeconomic status of the mother herself. The more time that highly educated mothers were with their kids—as opposed to sending them to day care and the like—the better those children did on cognitive tests. But for less educated mothers, kids did better when they went off to preschool and other structured activities. Hence the big effects of Head Start and other such programs that prepped low-income toddlers for K–12 schooling.

I didn't pay much attention to these studies until I found myself home with baby E. I am not one to talk aloud to my pets. I don't talk to myself, either. And I found talking to a baby made me feel just as ridiculous as if I were talking to my pet rock. Neither provided much in the way of response. I confessed to Natalie that I had nothing to say to baby E on the days she was away teaching.

"Just narrate what you are doing," she instructed. "Talk her through your day."

I tried. Honestly, I did. "Now Daddy's going to wash his face, first I lather up the soap, and then I put the bubbly foam on my cheeks. Then I splash water to rinse it all off, yay!" After one or two of these silly perorations, I would regress to my innate, taciturn state, like a dieter eventually returns to his natural eating habits and baseline weight.

"It's really critical for her verbal development!" Natalie would scold me. We were in a heightened state of anxiety about E, not only because she was our first child together, but because of her prematurity. By the time she was aged two and still not talking, our young-parent nervousness had metastasized into full-blown panic. I was doing my best to talk as much as I could; however, like most parents of young children, I was totally and utterly exhausted and could barely keep the needle above the poverty level. [3] I also suffered from a failure of imagination and really only knew how to do two things with toddlers: 1) play fetch (exactly like it sounds—I throw a ball or toy as if the kid were a dog and he or she brings it back and drops it at my feet); and 2) read.

Once kids get a little older, they can graduate from "fetch" to more complex activities. Here is Yo involved in one of our favorites: Houdini. What's great about this is not just that they really learn problem-solving skills, but that if you really tie them up well, you can get some time to do the dishes or the crossword puzzle while they struggle to get free. And if you do the muzzle right, you can get some peace and quiet for a few minutes as well. Note to child services: Yo asks to play this game; even his grandmother lobbied for her turn to be tied up when she visited.

The upshot was that I did nothing with them that involved my own physical movement. I was the human manatee parent. Many parents bake with their kids. They take them to museums. They throw the football around. They even build tree houses. I utterly failed as a parent on the quite important physical exercise front—delegating that domain of responsibility to their much more fun and athletically gifted mother and uncle. All I know how to do is read in bed. Plus, the fact that they were so close in age meant that for many years I could read the same thing to both kids aloud, perhaps alternating between a volume on sharks and a fairy book.[4]

Over the course of months and years of practice and refinement, I developed a particular style of reading aloud to them. Call it nerdish. It involves defining words along the way. In this manner, I could read texts to them that would seemingly be way over their grade level, rife with complex sentence structures and new words. So, for example, when they were very little, I read them a Beverly Cleary book meant for third graders, *Dear Mr. Henshaw*. A typical exchange: "Did she ever have pimples—" (I would interrupt the passage.) DO YOU KNOW WHAT PIMPLES ARE? (I would ask them.) "ZITS" ARE SLANG FOR PIMPLES. (I would have already defined "slang" in a broader discussion about what the difference between a dialect and a language is.) THESE ARE PIMPLES (and I'd point to my own teenage acne that seemed to still rear its head, so to speak, even into my thirties). EEEWWW! they would scream in unison. I guarantee they never needed the word "pimple" defined for them ever again.

Once the definition had sunk in, the reader would then repeat the entire clause or phrase: "Did she ever have pimples when she was a girl like the girl in her book, and what did it feel like to be a famous author?" AN "AUTHOR" IS A PERSON WHO HAS WRITTEN A BOOK OR OTHER TEXT, SO IT'S LIKE A WRITER. Then, since this was presumably new to the kids, I'd read the entire sentence over: "Did she ever have pimples"— "*Zits*," I might offer as a layer in a lower tone, as if I were a human thesaurus or a backup singer—"when she was a girl like the girl in her book and what did it feel like to be a famous author?" "*Writer*," I'd add in my linguistic echo.

I'd keep doing this all through the text until the kids were fed up and yelled at me, "We know what 'personality' means! Just read!"

Another time we had just finished reading the latest install-ment of *The Magic Treehouse* when I realized that they might not have known what the word "transplant" meant. Once I explained it to them, E asked, "Could you have a heart transplant?"

"Sure," I explained, wishing I could have had one myself as Yo wriggled on top of me, crushing my rib cage, all three of us squished into the bottom bunk. "Except that there aren't a lot of them since there aren't a lot of hearts from dead people that you can use. But I once knew someone who had a heart transplant," I bragged. "He was a sixty-year-old man with the heart of a twenty-year-old."

"So is he going to live extra-long now?" E asked.

"Actually he died already," I admitted. "But he lived a lot lon-ger than he would have if he never got the heart."

"Where do they get the hearts from?"

"From car accidents, mostly. They can't use hearts from old people. Sometimes they even use baboon hearts."

"Can you have a brain transplant?" she continued the line of questioning.

"Well," I paused. "That's not possible yet, but I am sure it will happen someday. Only it would be a body transplant. Not a brain transplant."

"What do you mean?" she asked while Yo listened, lying still for a change, perhaps out of fear from this eerie line of discussion.

"I mean that if we switched brains, then I would be in your body, and you would be in my body. Daddy would have the body of a five-year-old girl, and you would have the body of me. You would see out of my eyes."

"And I would talk with your voice?"

"That's right. Remember you are in your brain. It's our bodies we are switching."

"And . . ." Now Yo perked up. "What if we put my brain into the body of a baboon!"

"Yeah!" E got into this, too.

"Then I would be a baboon and a baboon would be Yo!"

"You would be trapped inside a baboon's body and not able to say what you want to say, because a baboon's voice box is not right for speaking English."

"And the human body would talk English like me, right?"

"No, silly." E asserted elder sibling authority. "The baboon brain would be trying to speak baboon using your voice. And it would try to swing with its tail when it doesn't have one."

I guarantee they never needed the word "transplant" explained to them again, even if they did suffer from simian nightmares for a stretch.

However, reading must be interactive beyond definitions,

synonyms, and word origins, which, by the way, are a great way to really encode the meaning solidly in their synapses. (I mean, how could they not love the story of the word "shampoo," which came from the Hindi word for head massage and wasn't introduced to dandruff-infested Britain until the nineteenth century by an Indian?)

Interactivity consisted in part of asking them whether they thought a certain metaphor worked for them, as in "dark as a sullen cloud before the sun" (Lord Byron, by the way). Or for alternatives—E's: "The sky stretched out like a great black cloak studded with diamonds." Yo's: "Dark as the inside of a reptile's ass." Interactivity also involved simply asking them what they thought the main character would do next. E and I were recently reading Jane Austen's *Pride and Prejudice*, and we spent the whole first part of the book changing our minds as to who the dour Mr. Darcy would end up falling in love with (don't tell us, we aren't done yet).

A collateral benefit of reading aloud is that it is the most soporific activity ever invented. So now, even when the kids aren't around, if I ever experience the rare inklings of insomnia, all I have to do is read something aloud to myself, which does make me feel kind of silly when I'm doing it, but then again, I'm alone, so who cares.

An option for the parent struck with a case of laryngitis or illiteracy or work that can't wait till morning is to download audiobooks and just play them out loud. The drawback to that approach is that the kids don't get all the SAT words defined for them along the way. Some scholars may argue that *not* knowing all the words in a sentence is sometimes good, as it forces those spongy brains to figure out the meaning from context. I beg to differ. A lack of vocabulary is the single biggest obstacle to taking on the challenge of deeper and more difficult texts, be they the "Rime of the Ancient Mariner" or a cell biology textbook.

And furthermore, English has, by far, the most words of any language by virtue of its merging Germanic roots with Latin ones and being otherwise open to neologisms and foreign influences, in contrast to, say, French, which puts up such linguistic walls to the outer world as to have to invent silly words like *ordinateur* to describe what the rest of the modern world calls "computer."[5] (Another important technique to help kids remember words and, in fact, to figure them out on their own, is to break down words you are defining for them into their Latin and Greek roots, since most of us typically don't get a classical education these days in school.)

Plus, the number of irregularities in English grammar probably exceeds any other Western language. It's been famously said that English is the easiest language to speak poorly (at least we don't have declensions, and verb conjugations are fairly simple)—but the hardest language to speak well. So our kids have their work cut out for them. Let's not expect them to figure out what everything means by themselves.

So imagine my joy when, on the fourth-grade high-stakes test, Yo scored at the top of his class on the English Language Arts statewide exam. By the end of fifth grade we had, at home, read

The Iliad and *The Odyssey*; almost every other Greek myth (Yo wanting to set up his own dozen Herculean tasks); O. Henry (when E would bring a tear to my eye by explaining that she would gladly shave her head to get me a present as the main character in "Gift of the Magi" does); Poe (with little Yo, terrified, clinging to me in bed as we finished "The Raven"); Coleridge; Twain; Hemingway; the complete works of Rudyard Kipling; lots of other adult fare that I had meant to read myself in high school or college but didn't; and, of course, all the standard kid stuff ranging from *Captain Underpants* to the *Harry Potter* series.

The joy of a top-notch fourth-grade score or a 99th percentile result on the eighth-grade exam was only the quantitative external validation. The real parental pride came any time the kids would spontaneously use a big word—like when, on the way home from school in fourth grade, Yo yelled, "I wish I could articulate how infuriated I am with E!" (before striking her—but let's just forget about the violence issue for now; I'll take it up in chapter 7).

Or when the fifth grader E countered: "Please, you have no boundaries, Yo! I need my autonomy!" This row, evidently, was all because one of them had revealed the other's crush to the entire schoolyard, so now everyone knew that E liked a boy named Spencer. Like I said, it wasn't always easy with them so close in age.

Or when E's memoiristic story about our family won a Gold Key and Best in Grade scholarship at the National Scholastic Art & Writing Awards and an editor thought it good enough to publish in a major national outlet.

In the end, however, it turns out that the original Hart and Risley study on word counts that—along with parental enervation—drove my whole approach to reading education was highly flawed. Most of the welfare families also happened to be black, while the scientific observers were white. So it was later hypothesized that the actual word counts among free-range humans are less divergent by social class than would appear. The large gaps were at least partially the result of a racially tinged white coat effect. Namely, the poor black families felt rather self-conscious speaking in front of the white researchers and clammed up. So the study taught us a little something about class differences in verbal achievement, just not what was intended. So maybe E would have scored her 99th percentile and her literary prize even if I had stayed quietly inside my own head. But at least I got to read many of the classics I was supposed to have read over the course of my own 1970–80s more feral development but never had.

5

Practicing the Delicate Arts of Extortion and Bribery (How *Else* Are American Children Supposed to Catch Up to the Finnish People in Math?)

IF YOU think I was focused on my kids' verbal skills, that's nothing compared to how much I obsessed about their math competence. In this case I wasn't pushing them on the basis of some flawed scientific research study, but because I, myself, had attended Stuyvesant, a highly competitive science and math high school. Alas, my motivation did not stem from having learned lots of math there—in fact, quite the opposite.

Here's the scene: In 1994, a fifteen-year-old student at Stuyvesant High School solves Fermat's last theorem in matrix algebra form.[1] National math, debate, and chess champions routinely come from the ranks of the student body. The Peglegs (yes, an unfortunate school mascot) boast more Nobel laureate graduates than all but a handful of colleges and universities, the country of Spain, and their bitter rival, the Bronx High School of Science. But there, in the front row of an eleventh-grade math class sits a twelfth grader who had squeaked into the school even though he had missed the cut-off by one point. This kid—me—somehow managed to take less than the minimum level of algebra and trigonometry required by the New York State Board of Regents and now had to make up for it in order to graduate.

Although Stuyvesant was a math and science high school, I found that one could get away with taking almost exclusively analytic philosophy, film studies, and history classes, shunning all but a minimum of biology, chemistry, and geometry—not to mention the one or *two* years of calculus that most of my classmates endured. Back then, in the wet-n-wild 1980s of hair gel, mousse, and crimping, how was I supposed to know that you had to start with Algebra I in eighth grade in order to make enough progress to take calculus in high school? Math, in other words, required a Soviet-style five-year plan and a Stalinesque parent to enforce it. My friends' parents seemed to know this, but mine didn't. So I took what classes appealed to me, reading Freud and Kant (or rather skimming them), watching Italian neorealist movies, and writing a science fiction novel while programming BASIC on my friend's Sinclair ZX80 computer in between hanging out at Julian's pool hall and playing basketball after school.

My parents may not have paid much attention to what classes I was taking, but eventually the guidance counselor did, which is how I found myself seated in front of a future movie actress in, what was for me, remedial math. Back in 1985, Heather Juergensen was a blonde—though in her biggest movie role, the lead of *Kissing Jessica Stein* in 2001, she was cast as a gorgeous brunette lipstick lesbian. The point of mentioning Heather is that I could hardly concentrate during third period and barely learned enough of the material to pass the class, let alone be prepared for calculus when I got to Berkeley. This is just one of the sort of random events that can affect a student's trajectory. And when it happens in a subject that builds as sequentially as math does, it can have enormous ripple effects down the line. When sociologists talk about "luck," "chance," or their "error term," Heather Juergensen sitting behind you in math class is the kind of thing they mean.

This math deficit would continue to haunt me for the rest of my career as a scientist. The moment one or another statistician was running through their so-called models—argot for equations filled with Greek letters, exponents, and calculus signifiers—I would seize up with a vestigial panic from high school trigonometry, equal parts Heather-induced sexual inadequacy and mathematical underpreparation. Same is true for when I, myself, need to *teach* statistics to graduate students. I fear that I'm going to forget everything the moment I start writing formulae on the board, even though I've taught the same course for years now. Simply put, I've been treading water with respect to numeracy ever since senior year.

No way was I going to let my kids suffer my fate. I really

amped up the math prep early in their elementary school years after a disturbing encounter when I saw that the son of economist colleagues could do cube roots and figure out large number divisions in his head. I had never emphasized numerical operations in our house. I had figured that times tables fell into the same category as the mechanics of reading: it was the conceptual aspects of math that were important, not the rote nuts and bolts that kids memorized in classrooms in Korea and Singapore (where they scored among the highest in international tests). As with decoding words, I told myself that there was no way that they would get to age ten and not know what six times six was (even if my mother failed when asked). Of course, unlike with verbal ability, I had no knowledge of any research that supported my intuition. Still, I had assumed that numeric fluency would come naturally, like learning the days of the week or the months of the year.[2] But when young Giovanni rattled off the formula for the area of a triangle, I got mad. Real mad.

So what if his parents were both economists—the most mathematically sophisticated social science? I may have barely passed trigonometry, but I aced the logic training that was part of the analytic philosophy classes I took.

Panicked that my kids were being left behind in the knowledge economy, I assuaged my anxiety by posing logic riddles to humiliate Giovanni and show off my kids' talents. "If John is taller than Joe, and Joe is taller than Murray, and Murray is shorter than Sam—" Here I paused to puff some air in and out of my mouth quickly to cool the mozzarella burn I had given myself on the roof of my mouth. I had charred my palate by scarfing the steaming pizza down my gullet before it had cooled sufficiently— failing my own version of the marshmallow, impulse-control test.

"Who's taller, John or Sam?"

"John is the tallest!" Giovanni shouted out before either of my kids could weigh in.

"No," E and Yo responded in unison. Then E shifted to her sweet maternal tone and turned to Giovanni: "We can't tell who's taller; all we know is that John and Sam are both taller than Murray, but either of them could be taller than the other. There's not enough information."

The Italian boy's mother was up at the counter getting another slice, so she didn't see me test her child or beam my competitively proud smile at the result. But, I wondered, maybe he was at a disadvantage for not having been a native English speaker. So I decided to sneak in another logic riddle before she returned with his dinner—one that relied more on numbers and less on names:

"You are at a river with a five-gallon jug and a three-gallon jug, but you need one gallon of water. How do you do it?" Giovanni shrugged his shoulders, but my kids jumped up and down in excited sibling rivalry to see who could figure it out fastest.

"I got it!" E yelled out.

"No," Yo swatted her raised hand down. "I got it."

They started bickering, and I had to calm them down by saying they could each whisper their answer to me independently. They each got it right. (You fill the three-gallon jug, pour its contents into the five-gallon jug, then do it a second time, and when you've filled the five-gallon jug, one gallon remains in the three-gallon jug.) I felt relieved that at least my kids had some skills this Rain Man kid didn't—even if neither E nor Yo had successfully memorized their times tables yet. (I immediately felt terribly guilty for trying to competitively crush this sweet little friend of theirs while his mother was getting oregano from the counter, so I atoned by going through a couple more examples with him so he would catch on. And he caught on, I must say, pretty darn fast.)

I vowed that my kids were never going to be left adrift in a sea of numbers like I had been. No, we were going to do extra math exercises every day, even if it killed me or them. I signed them up for an online course offered by Stanford University. It was expensive, but math, I reckoned, was something that had only grown in importance since 1985, when Heather had unintentionally waged her successful ground war for my attention. However, when E and Yo challenged me about the utility of doing set theory or probability on their school vacation, I didn't really have much in the way of an answer:

"It teaches you abstract concepts!" I stammered.

"I already know how to figure out tax on a bill or the right tip," E countered, for in gender-stereotypical manner, it was she who resisted math and Yo who hated writing. "I don't see why I need to ever talk about congruent angles. You don't use geometry, do you?"

"Well, no, but that doesn't matter. Maybe you want to be an architect? Huh? What then?" Actually, I figured that architects just relied on computer-aided design to do all the calculations for them, but I didn't, of course, share this information with her.

"I'll give you one gummy bear for each problem you do," I floundered. "Or twenty minutes of computer time for twenty minutes of math. Your choice."

"Both," she countered. We settled on a minute of gaming per minute of math in addition to a gummy bear for each two problems she completed correctly.

Soon math problems—not money—became the universal currency in our household. I figured that while with reading the main goal was to kick-start a lifelong love affair with books— i.e. generate intrinsic motivation to read often—almost nobody liked doing math, so bribery was in order.

I institutionalized this gummy bear/computer time formula, based on my understanding of the social-psychological literature on motivation—the sum total of which I had acquired in the weight room of the Columbia University gymnasium. I learned this from my workout partner during graduate school, James Yatish Shah (he doesn't actually use his middle name, but I think it's so cool sounding that I will). Jim is a social psychologist who studied goals system theory. In between reps at the bench press, Jim explained to me that there were two wellsprings of motivation: the ideal-self and the ought-self. These roughly corresponded to that which we want to do and that which we feel we need or are obligated to do.

Now a Duke University professor, Jim had spent his years in graduate school devising experiments to alternatively activate the ideal-self and the ought-self in his subjects as they solved anagrams for a token monetary payment. Along with which self was driving these poor undergraduates, Jim and his advisor also varied whether the task was simple or complex (i.e. multistep) and whether or not the students started with a pot of money and lost some for each wrong answer (that is, were faced with a punitive motivational system) or, alternatively, started with nothing and earned a payment for each correct answer (a reward-based approach).

To boil a lifetime's worth of research down to a couple sentences, what they found was the following: on average, Columbia undergraduate psychology students performed simple tasks better when they were put in an "ought-self" situation and motivated by the threat of punishment (i.e. loss-avoidance). But for complicated tasks, activating the ideal-self motivation while providing a reward system was more effective.

I took this to mean that if I wanted to work up to bench-pressing 125 percent of my weight, then I would best accomplish that by having Jim whip me each time I failed to complete a rep. But if I wanted to learn matrix algebra, some chocolate at the end of a successful quiz result was the way to go. Therefore, if I wanted to make E and Yo commit their times tables to memory, I needed to stand over them with a pin and give them a little prick every time they made an error. But since I actually was sticking to the notion that times tables would come on their own (along with typing, thanks to their desire to chat on Facebook) and I was more concerned about them learning the deeper concepts of the

Koch snowflake, the Fibonacci sequence, the difference between the median, mean, and mode, and other fun stuff, I needed to work on positive reinforcement and to hope that through association with candy, money, or computer games, math would somehow appeal to their ideal-selves with which they would kick more quantitative butt.

The only problem was that Jim also found that the more effective method of reinforcement (positive or negative) depended on the person herself. If someone was more driven by their ought-self in life—as hyperresponsible, guilt-prone, firstborn E was—then threat of loss works best (i.e. negative reinforcement). However, if someone is driven by their ideal-self motivation system—i.e. seeking rewards, as embodied by my hedonistic, obsessive, guilt-free second-born son—then the positive reward system functions best. I couldn't very well run two separate systems in my house. It was exhausting enough carrying out one. So I went with the research that broke the effectiveness of the motivation system by the complexity of the task to be performed and set it up as a positive, cumulative approach. That is, they started at zero but earned gummy bears or computer time or money starting with each math problem rather than offering them, say, twenty minutes of computer time and taking it away for each problem they *didn't* do.

The result was that the math problem became the smallest universal denomination of coinage in our realm. Dimes, quarters, dollars, and Sour Patch Kids were merely the reward purchased by having computed the area of a triangle. Likewise, that same geometry solution could also produce two extra minutes of *World of Warcraft* gaming time. My bigger worry with my system was not how it was working in the present moment, but what the implications were for the long term. For as much as I was getting decent short-term results with my bribery approach, I worried about another aspect of psychological research with which I had become familiar: the difference between intrinsic motivation and extrinsic motivation.

These sources of motivation can overlap with—but are ultimately conceptually distinct from—the ideal- and ought-selves I mentioned above. For example, you can be extrinsically and ought-self–motivated to perform a task if you are fearful of letting someone else down. You can be intrinsically motivated to have a hot girlfriend because you are an aesthete and place a high value on the pleasantness of a woman's figure to your eye. Or, extrinsically you may get a rise out of impressing your friends that you are an alpha male who can attract such a fine, foxy mama. And, of course, you can be intrinsically ought-self–motivated if, for example, you are a workaholic.

The reward system for math allowed me to vary some other conditions as well. Most notably, I tried to instill an ability to delay gratification by varying the time scale of the rewards. "You can each have twenty minutes of computer time now," I offered one evening when it had gotten kind of late, and they had both done a math session. "You've earned it. But if you wait till morning, then you can have forty minutes."

"You're just hoping we'll forget and then lose all our time!"

"I'm not, I promise." I reached into the pen drawer to pull out a marker and a pad of yellow Post-its. "See, I'll even put up a note that reminds us that you both have forty minutes coming." They countered that I would just destroy the notes while they slept. I hadn't anticipated this sort of trust issue in our negotiations. "Look, you can put the IOU in your safes." I had bought them each a money box with a lock—mainly to prevent Yo and the neighbor kid from dipping into the savings E had managed to accumulate.

"Then we'll forget about it," E argued back. We finally came up with the idea that we'd put both a Post-it note on the refrigerator in plain view so we'd remember and a separate, date-stamped IOU in their safe, which they would redeem. Somewhere along the way, however, the price got raised to forty minutes of bonus for the twelve-hour delay, resulting in a total of one hour they would be able to play the next morning. I didn't care; it was worth not having them exposed to screens that late at night, which would have thrown off their entire sleep schedule according to some recent studies by pediatricians. The next day was Saturday, so they'd have plenty of time to get their hour in and still be able to do another math session.

Later that year I offered them a hundred twenty dollars to go without candy or other sweets for a whole year. Twenty up front; another forty at the six-month mark; and the final sixty upon completion of the year. Soon I was offering them all sorts of deals in my attempt to extend their time horizons. I succeeded; on the candy front they were, in fact, able to make it the entire year without sweets. But I didn't do so well on extending their time horizon, which is known as the discount rate. That rate is what someone needs to pay you in order for you to defer receipt of a payment. In business transactions, the discount rate is usually figured around 4 percent annually—higher or lower depending on the term length, the inflation rate, and bond yields. When it came to deferring gratification, my kids were more like bail bond loan sharks or some small African nation with hyperinflation. I had to pay them essentially a 50 to 100 percent interest rate daily.

This had me very worried, since I had recently become obsessed with psychologist Walter Mischel's marshmallow test (see chapter 3) and subsequent research showing that the ability to delay gratification—i.e. a low discount rate—was highly predictive of future success. This research made me *extremely* nervous about Yo. The kid was extremely now-oriented, to put it mildly. He was so shortsighted as to be "past-oriented." If caught in the middle of a *World of Warcraft* dungeon (or, at an earlier age, on a Pokémon quest), Yo would mortgage his future home and give away his firstborn just to score a few more minutes of computer time.

"Just t-ten more minutes," he'd stutter as he stiff-armed me with one hand and navigated his flying dragon with the other. "I promise I'll do double math tomorrow. Please. Please, I just have to finish this dungeon. The other players will be so mad at me if I leave now."

"Folks must lose their internet connection and cut out of missions all the time," I offered weakly by way of retort.

"Dad, please! This is the last boss to defeat. Then we get the treasure."

I inched closer to him, putting my palm over the edge of the laptop screen before slowly folding it down.

"Okay, double math tomorrow!" he yelled now in his panic. "And I'll do double math all next week, too!" He was demonstrating what economists called hyperbolic discounting, and frankly, it scared me. The idea of hyperbolic discounting is that while everyone should value present rewards greater than future rewards (at the very least for the reason that it's never 100 percent certain that we will be around to enjoy them given the inherent uncertainty of human life), folks actually demonstrate a huge present bias. So, for example, given the choice between fifty dollars now and seventy dollars in a month, many folks will take the fifty dollars now. But given what should amount to an equivalent choice—seventy dollars in thirteen months or fifty dollars in a year—folks will delay the gratification and take the seventy dollars. What this means, in essence, is that there is one's future self—who will be rational and reasonable—and then there is the present self: a nut like Yo who would trade anything for another ten minutes of WOW-time or an extra hit on the crack pipe. In fact, in experiments, addicted mice demonstrated much steeper discount rates (i.e. behaved like Yo) than nonaddicted mice. There's no question that addiction causes this extremely present-oriented state. But it's more of an open debate as to whether "innate" differences in discount rates lead to varying probabilities of getting addicted in the first place. Likewise, folks who are nonaddicts have a poor understanding about how greatly their future addicted selves will value that marginal cigarette; that's, in fact, the trap of addiction, since the act of smoking each cigarette not only gives pleasure in that moment, it changes the very equation inside us as to what is pleasurable.

"Okay," I sighed, agreeing to his offer. I wasn't making much progress in lowering his discount rate or resolving his time inconsistency. So I might as well use his irrationalities to my own advantage by forcing him to do more math as part of the bargaining between his present and future selves. I only hoped that the academic research pendulum would swing back so that cognitive skills would be seen to trump the set of non-cognitive skills that were all the rage right now.

Of course, his dungeon ended up taking a lot more than ten minutes, and by the time he wound down from the high of having completed a level-20 adventure (evidently, a first for him) and actually fell asleep, it was 12:30 a.m. Lying awake next to him in bed after he finally drifted off, I quelled my visions of Yo in a crack house by reminding myself that he also became intensely focused when it came to nondigital, nondopamine-based activities like building models or doing science experiments. And that, at least, was supposed to be good, according to another psychologist, Mihaly Czikszentmihalyi, who referred to that zoned-out, tuned-in state as "flow" and advised everyone from teachers to CEOs on how to achieve it among their students and workers. Yo's intensity was a double-edged sword. I just had to figure out how to help him deploy it for productive activities rather than destructive ones.

Perhaps I had gone a little too far in my quantification and marketization of my kids' lives. I hope they don't feel like I somehow objectified them through market exchange, as Karl Marx might have argued. What's more, I soon learned that my approach might not have been as effective as I had hoped. My reward system had been based on a social experiment called Progresa-Oportunidades (Progress-Opportunities). Economists (they have all the fun) went down to Mexico and randomly picked some villages to which to apply their "treatment" while documenting control villages to follow for comparison purposes. The so-called treatment was to pay families for doing right by their kids. So, for example, a family might get 10 pesos for bringing their child in to get a vaccination. Or they might get 100 pesos for making sure their daughter attended school regularly (since daughters were the ones who were often encouraged to drop out of school early to help out at home). The kids themselves could earn money as well by passing classes and tests.

The Progresa experiment was such a success that it was cancelled partway through because the skipped-over communities (the control villages) demanded to be included as well. (A similar thing happened in sub-Saharan Africa during a randomized trial of male circumcision as an approach to stem the spread of AIDS; it was so effective that it was deemed unethical to deny the treatment to anyone, so the idea of a control group was scrapped after the initial data came in.)[3] So, the experiment was converted to the social program Oportunidades and expanded to cover the entire country.

The results were so exciting that when New York's Mayor

Bloomberg got wind of them, he launched a similar scheme in our very own city. Only problem was that something got lost in translation north of the border. The results for New York City were disappointing, to say the least.

In the back room of an Italian restaurant in—of all places—Madison, Wisconsin, I watched the graphs flicker across the screen as we ate what passes for tiramisu in the American heartland. After millions of dollars of private investment (much of it reportedly coming from Bloomberg himself) and several years of trials in the public school system led by Harvard economics prodigy Roland Fryer, the verdict had been rendered by an independent policy evaluation firm with the macho name of Manpower Research Demonstration Corporation. And the upshot was a big fat zero. No matter how they sliced and diced the data, there really was no return on investment for the treatment of paying kids (and parents) for doing better in school. Fryer had tried to motivate them all sorts of different ways. Some kids got the rewards if they, themselves, met certain targets. Others had to succeed as a group—a twist that was meant to invoke the esprit de corps of Parris Island Marine Corps basic training where the entire platoon has to do pushups if a single recruit fails to polish his boots and gun adequately. The only problem with New York teenagers was that it was a reward-based system rather than a punitive one. So the kids probably figured—perhaps rightly—that there would be a shirker or two who would bring down the whole group and thus, why bother trying extra hard themselves only to be disappointed by their peers?

My conference dinner compatriots devoured these new data with the same voraciousness that they ingested their desserts. I was one of a few sociologists trying to fit in with the bespectacled economists that dominated this annual policy research lollapalooza. As these practitioners of the dismal science asked whether there were perhaps heterogeneous treatment effects that had gone undetected (i.e. that there were positive effects for particular subgroups like black female students that got washed out in the overall analysis), or attenuation bias due to measurement error (too much noise in the data), or selective attrition (whether the folks who responded well to the rewards might have disproportionately been lost to the evaluators for follow-up), I obsessed over what this all meant for my home-based Oportunidades mini scheme. Perhaps it was time for some reevaluation of my bribery approach in light of the Manpower results. After (co-)sleeping on it, I decided to stick with the plan. My decision was reinforced subsequently upon reading a study by the economist C. Kirabo Jackson, which found that paying high school students (and their teachers) for getting passing scores on AP exams did, in fact, result in performance gains and a positive effect that lasted all the way through college to the labor market. So maybe all I needed to do was reward myself, too, in my role as "teacher"?

Anyway, new study or no new study, what choice did I have? I had probably already eroded their intrinsic motivation by then, so what now? I needed to keep up the maintenance dose of gummy bears and video gaming in order to maintain their performance till they graduated, lest they experience math withdrawal effects and do worse on their SATs. It was a textbook case of path dependence.

Ah well, perhaps I should just relax. There seems to be a paradox about math education anyway. On the one hand, many folks in the lower income brackets need more basic skills—called "shop math." There's a dearth of blue collar workers who can manipulate fractions and solve word problems that come up in service sector and manufacturing jobs—like figuring out how many pallets they will need to move a certain load given the weight and the tonnage restrictions for each pallet. This is really a problem for the elementary and middle schools to solve. But when we get to so-called higher math, from algebra onward, things start to get muddled.

Very few professions require their practitioners to solve polynomial equations—let alone differential equations. (Those talents, however, do pretty much guarantee employability in today's economy, especially if mixed with some computer programming skills.) Yet aspiring doctors, nurses, and a host of other professional people are required to jump through trigonometry (and sometimes even calculus) hoops to gain entry, despite never needing to take a first derivative in their entire career trajectory. That is, for highly selective colleges and careers, math is often used as a weeding mechanism. It's simply hard; so requiring one to slog through it is a good test of those good old non-cognitive skills.

So it should come as no surprise that kids who score high on math at pretty much any age are more likely to graduate high school and college alike. And they go on to earn better wages than their lower-scoring counterparts—even when factoring out IQ (which, as we know, is poorly measured, thus leaving lots of room for other things to matter). And disadvantaged kids who receive quality math tutoring show gains in achievement and educational completion. So math scores may be picking up perseverance and self-discipline as much as native mathematical ability. Perhaps all kids need is something really mentally taxing—writing a novel, studying ancient Greek, philology, or analytic philosophy—in order to develop the generic mental skills for success. Or maybe they don't. Maybe they just need to be encouraged to pursue whatever they like doing, other than video games, that is.

The sociologist Andrew Hacker has argued, for example, that we lose a lot of bright kids thanks to algebra—kids who might excel in other, more humanistic areas if they weren't dashed by this math requirement. Indeed, studies show that when tougher standards for eighth-grade math are implemented, lower income kids suffer in their achievement and their graduation rates; they tend to perform more poorly, get discouraged, and drop out. Even someone as snobby as former treasury secretary and Harvard president Larry Summers has argued that our math curricula are outdated: we make students learn geometry and trigonometry that was useful when we were mostly farmers concerned with plot acreages; today, he suggests, we should instill a better understanding of probability and statistics.

Since I can't change the system alone, I am going to go with the odds and hold the gummy bears and the stick over my kids. When they have jumped through enough hoops as to not have closed off any major career choices, I can remove the extrinsic motivation, and if their intrinsic math motivation vanishes— then starving poets they may be! Or, if they prefer, they can continue to live on gummy bears and algebra problems. Because, what is a paycheck, after all, if not the ultimate form of extrinsic motivation?

Truth be told, I don't think my mini economy has altered their internal goal equilibrium one bit. Rather, gender seems to be the primary driver in their academic passions. True to stereotypes, as they approached adolescence, E dove deeper and deeper into books and literature and became increasingly less interested in mathematics. Yo presented the exact mirror image. He began to research multidimensional geometry and fractals—on his own time, no less. But convincing him to read any one of the twenty-five independent reading books he was supposed to have completed during a given school year was about as difficult as getting him to crawl on his hands and knees to see the Virgin of Guadalupe. For him, reading was a necessary evil that merely served as a means to an end—namely, a way to obtain information. He was hardly interested in the narratives of novels anymore. Rather, he preferred to read articles about the fall of Rome or the engineering of suspension bridges. Better still, he'd rather watch a documentary to take in what he wanted to know about quantum mechanics or, say, the chemistry of explosives.

Thus, I had plied one academic arena (math) with extrinsic

rewards and left another (reading) devoid of such contamination, but in the end, the presence or absence of a reward system did little to affect their passion for the subject matter. Of course, I can't know whether I would have ended up with a son passionate for literature had I paid him by the page. Or a daughter who lived for geometry had I not introduced payment for polynomials. But I'm guessing—rather unscientifically, I should add—that it would have made little difference in either case.

6

GET THEM THE PUPPY!
GET THEM THE PUPPY!

LIKE ME, Yo constantly fidgeted, which made eating at a restaurant quite challenging. As a result, we usually only ate at proper restaurants with place settings and table service when it was necessary because we were on the road, having dragged the kids along to some academic conference, or perhaps, visiting relatives. Thus, by the time we made it to a restaurant, the kids were usually tired from walking and quite hungry to boot, which made sitting still all the more difficult. This time in Australia was no different. Yo had been unable to sit still while waiting for our food, so when he tried to saw the table with his butter knife, I deployed one of the tactics my grandfather had used on me, taking him on a tour of the beach-side restaurant in between courses.

When Yo espied a tank of crabs and lobsters, he announced, "Cool, look at the pets they have here! I wish we had some pet lobsters; can we get some when we're back home?" Before I could answer him, he noticed the tight rubber bands around their claws. "Is that so that they don't attack each other?" his finger hyperextended against the greasy glass as he pointed to the bondage implements. "Oh, you know, when lobsters wave, it's to show dominance—who's got the bigger claw."

I should have kept my mouth shut, but I followed my tradition of bursting bubbles and announced, "Those are so that the lobsters don't snap at the waiters when they reach in to grab them."

"Wait." His face dropped, and his finger smeared down the glass as his arm fell. "These are for eating here?"

"Yes, darling," I explained. "This is a seafood restaurant."

"No," he said. "Can we get them? We have to save them. We have to! We can release them at the beach or in the river out back! Please!?" He was running back and forth in front of the tank as if he were a dog trying to get at the aquatic creatures. "Please buy them."

Of course Natalie, the professional empathizer, supported Yo's plan. So, we asked to order two lobsters at $45 each—a pretty expensive ransom, if you ask me. As the staff were reaching in the tank to retrieve them, I confessed that we wanted them alive.

"Sorry, sir," the waitress explained. "We can't sell them to you like that. We have to cook them."

"What do you mean you can't sell them to us like that?"

"It's illegal for us to sell pets; we are only licensed to sell food."

"Okay. Well I want to order two lobsters to go; I want them cooked so rare that they are, in fact, raw. So you don't need to cook them at all. I want them alive on my plate."

"We don't do takeaway," she countered, using the Australianism for take-out.

"Okay, then we'll have lobster *très* tartar to stay."

"We cannot do that. I'm very sorry."

Yo wanted to steal them and leave the money wedged under the tank, but I convinced him that we'd go to the fish market the next morning and liberate four lobsters for the price of these two here, who would have to be sacrificed for the greater good. That calmed him down enough, though I had a tough time peeling both kids away from the glass when it was time to leave that night, and they hadn't really eaten any of their (vegetarian) dinner. "We'll never see those lobsters again," E narrated in the car ride home. "Those unique lives—gone. Just think how that lobster's mother felt when her child got trapped in the underwater cage and yanked out to go die at some restaurant. Just so someone can have flesh that tastes good when there's so much else to eat." I thought of interrupting to explain that perhaps lobsters don't actually have a high degree of parental investment or maternal care but decided against it.

"Shut up, E!" Yo covered his ears to spare his brain the imagery she was conjuring. She flashed a sly grin.

Certain kids are machine/vehicle kids and other kids are

animal kids. Both E and Yo were so far on the animal side of the spectrum that it's surprising that they didn't sprout wings and tails. Yo's favorite game to play during the Oedipal stage was "big buck with antlers," which involved the two of us rearing up on our hind legs and smashing into each other on our king-sized family bed in competition for the doe. Neither kid had much interest in trains, trucks, or backhoes. The vehicles and heavy machinery that fascinated their cousins failed to capture their imaginations. Meanwhile, E at age seven decided on her own to become a vegetarian. Yo also tried forsaking meat, but eventually succumbed to bacon, the gastronomic Achilles' heel of all boys with Jewish blood. Though he ate flesh, he continued to devote hours of his free time to memorizing species, family, and genus of animals both extant and extinct. I must have read the book about ancient megaladon sharks to him more than a hundred times. So much so that "megaladon" became slang for "huge" in our household, though it never really seemed to catch on in his preschool.

Our would-be lobster tartar dinner had been our goodbye meal with the "rellies" Down Under. The next day we were to depart Brisbane for New York and the start of the new semester. The plan had been to swing by the fish market in the morning before heading out to the airport, but we ended up sleeping in late; and packing took a long time, not to mention saying goodbye yet again to the endless number of aunts and uncles whom the kids enjoyed down there, so we didn't have time to put our crustacean liberation plan into action.

Besides a lot of tears, the result was that when we got back home, the kids used this broken promise of animal rescue as leverage to argue for new pets: guinea pigs. Never mind that we already lived with two rescue cats, a yappy little Yorkie dog, two lizards, numerous fish, and a rabbit that resided on our back deck (which had been dumped on us by a classmate of E's whose two dads were too fastidious to allow this particular *Leporidae* to remain with them). And that was only the current batch of non-humans with which we coresided. Over the years, we had enjoyed (or suffered) the graces of a bullfrog,[1] a prior dog, goldfish (large, koi-sized as well as small fish tank variety), drunk mice,[2] parakeets (cage-free), feral, rescued pigeons (ditto), mourning doves (ditto), two other rabbits, brain-damaged rats (rescued from the NYU neural science department), salamanders, red-eared slider turtles, snakes, sugar gliders (an Australian marsupial that looks like a squirrel but has a forked penis), weever fish, and zebra finches (again, flying free in the apartment).

I was determined to hold the line on any more humans or nonhumans joining our ranks. So I mumbled something about discussing it with their mother and then shepherded them away from the glass tanks at Petland Discounts on 23rd Street, full of multicolored little rodents that looked like experiments in Mendelian crosses. Some were pure black, some brown, some mosaic; meanwhile some had short hair, others long. Yo favored a tufty mix that looked like a fuzzy quilt that had been haphazardly stitched together. For some reason he called this one the "Arab." E, meanwhile, was busy shooing bully pigs away from a black one that cowered in the corner, his ears chewed full of holes from the abuse he endured thanks to his position as the omega at the bottom of the pecking order.

I seemed to have succeeded in diverting their attention long enough for them to forget about the guinea pigs once school started up again, but the next weekend I needed to call on the kids for their assistance. Our toilet was backed up, and neither Drano nor borrowing the superintendent's snake did the trick. We had to take the toilet off the wall, where it was mounted, and flush out the waste pipe with water. Then I had to squeeze my hand down the three-inch-wide pipe. I mention this detail because the pipe's width was, in fact, part of the problem and key to the story: Building code requires the pipe to be four inches, but our shady plumber had skimped and saved money by using the narrower version. And now, it turned out, we were living with the consequences, since a plastic mini bottle of shampoo had gotten flushed down the toilet and wedged itself right where there was an S-shaped bend in the outflow pipe.

(Personally, I blame my sister since she, as a Purell devotee, refuses to sit on our toilet so as to avoid exposure to our germs. She probably knocked it in during one of her awkward bathroom squats at our house.)

I managed to wriggle my hand down and grasp the offending plastic item with the tips of my fingers, but, as you might imagine, it was very slippery given what it was coated with. So every time I tried to remove it, my grasp failed, and all I pulled out were scraped-up, feces-covered knuckles. Finally, I gave up and poured rubbing alcohol on my open wounds—praying to

God that I didn't end up with some sort of deadly *E. coli* infection. It was a job for a child, I realized, as my mind flashed to Steven Spielberg's film *Schindler's List*, where the title character convinced the Nazis to spare Jewish children by claiming to need them to polish the inside of shell casings, since only their little fingers could fit inside.

"E," I yelled. "Come here please!" Yo was lucky enough to be away on a play date.

"What is it?"

"I need you to wriggle your hand inside this pipe and pull out whatever is blocking it. It's something plastic," I added, just so she didn't think that I was asking her to pull out a turd. I personally made a big distinction between a piece of shit, per se, and something covered in crap.

"Um, why me?" she countered, and before I could respond, she also asked, "Where are the gloves?"

"There're no gloves. Gloves won't work, and my hands won't work because I can't get a grip. I need your smaller fingers."

"I can't just stick my bare hand in there!"

"Yes, you can. You will," I was trying to be all patriarchal and whatnot.

"No way." She wasn't going for my macho act.

"Okay," I reasoned, resorting to my default bribery approach. "I'll pay you twenty dollars."

She stood her ground. "No." Now, had I been dealing with Yo, we would have implicitly passed the first line of the old joke where a man offers a lady in a bar a million dollars to have sex with him, and when she agrees, he instead suggests a mere ten dollars. Offended, she refuses, asking rhetorically, "What kind of girl do you take me for?" He answers that when she agreed to do it for a million, he already knew what kind of girl she was, but now they were just haggling about the price. For Yo, there was a price for everything—and it was never the first price offered. Dealing with him was both as straightforward and as exhausting as cutting a deal with a carpet seller in a Turkish bazaar. E was an entirely different story. Money held no appeal for her. In fact, on the couple of occasions when she found a five-dollar bill on the street, she handed it over to the first homeless person she saw. When we were robbed and she lost her life savings, she announced, "Oh well, they probably needed it more than we did." I won't be surprised if she takes a vow of poverty and actually carries out her childhood fantasy of living with the chimpanzees in Africa, Jane Goodall–style.

She desired no material goods, so threatening her with loss of funds or rewarding her with pecuniary promises never worked.

"Just do it!" I stammered.

"I can't do it."

I was in crisis mode. I simply couldn't give in and pay to get a professional plumber in, especially on a Sunday, especially when we knew what the problem was and were so close to solving it on our own. Maybe it was a bit of a wannabe-manly-Dad effect— wanting to prove that I could solve a plumbing problem on my own (or almost on my own). "Okay," I pleaded, "fifty bucks."

"No."

"What kind of spoiled children have I raised?" I yelled now. "I can't believe what a spoiled brat you are!"

"I am not spoiled!" This really got to her. "I am not spoiled because I won't stick my hand into a pipe of poo."

"Fine, don't then." I pouted and turned away, as if I were a cross six-year-old. "Go play your computer games while I deal with this shit, literally. I can't believe how spoiled you are. I didn't think you were this way, but I guess I was wrong."

She left the bathroom as I squatted again to try to wiggle my forearm down the dirty passageway, asking myself what Freud would say about the father-daughter interaction around this symbolic task. Meanwhile, I knew my manipulative little tantrum would do the trick in activating her guilt circuits. Sure enough, in ten minutes she was back. "Okay," she said as she squatted down. "I am not spoiled!" She added and glared at me.

"I know you're not spoiled, darling," I began before she interrupted me.

"Yo is spoiled. I'm not."

Though I knew she was looking for me to agree with her and say aloud that her brother was indeed spoiled, I stayed quiet, and she finally bunched up her fingers as if to make a hand shadow of a bird's beak and guided her hand into the intestinal pipe. "Ewww! Ewwww! Ewwwwww!" she said louder each time, followed by explicitly fake crying. "This is so gross!"

"Can you feel it?"

"Yes, but it keeps slipping out of my fingers each time I try to pull it around the bend."

Instructions for preventing spoiled offspring and/or childhood allergies: 1. Flush small plastic object down this device. 2. Require child to reach down and get it. 3. Don't repeat even if necessary.

She gave it a couple more tries and then gave up. Finally, the plumber came and poured some highly toxic compound down the open sewer and it melted the plastic, releasing some toxic smoke in the process. I made sure E was back in her room with the door closed and window opened so she wouldn't get a lungful of the carcinogen.

Later we were reading J. D. Salinger in bed, and she said, "I can't believe you called your own daughter spoiled. And I can't believe you bullied me into sticking my arm down the drain."

I kissed her on top of her head. "I'm sorry, sweetheart; I know you are the furthest thing from spoiled. And I'm so proud of you. Just think how you'll be able to tell your own kids someday how rough it was for you and how easy they have it not having to fish objects out of the sewage." I still felt bad that she had gotten stuck with the dirty job, so after a few more pages of *Catcher in the Rye* I suddenly blurted out—as if I had been under torture— "Okay, okay, you can have a guinea pig."

To rationalize going back on my line in the mulch, I told myself that living among/with animals was good for them, as recent science had begun to reveal. Several studies had been issued suggesting that contrary to past wisdom, living with pets actually reduced rates of childhood allergies and asthma. It made complete sense to me given what I knew about the so-called "hygiene hypothesis." That is, one of the current theories in the steep rise in the rates of various childhood allergies and other autoimmune diseases (such as type 1 diabetes, inflammatory bowel syndrome, multiple sclerosis, and possibly even autism) is the fact that things have gotten much cleaner these days and thus our immune systems don't get enough of a workout from living among open sewers and cow dung.

This hygiene hypothesis comes in several flavors. One is that by not getting exposed to enough infectious agents, we don't "learn" to deploy regulator T-cells to suppress T1 and T2 cell responses, which, in turn, attack harmless proteins like those found in peanuts or pollen. A slight variant suggests that our T2s generate antibodies against things they shouldn't attack because we don't give our T1 cells enough of a workout. T1-mediated responses involve white blood cells attacking invaders, and the T2 pathway protects us by generating antibodies (proteins) that bind to the uninvited guests. These knock down the putative invasive species, and in the process, suppress T1 responses. When we don't give our T1 cells something to chew on, so to speak, they turn against us.

This is ostensibly one of the reasons why many hippy-dippy parents are against vaccinating their kids (even if they aren't actually aware of the scientific rationale).[3] Getting chicken pox itself gives your entire immune system a run for its money. But getting the varicella vaccine merely prepares the antibody recipe so that you can knock down any future virus before it can get established in your cells and really make you sick. In other words, the vaccine trains the T2 response at the expense of the T1 response.

I personally think that saying goodbye to smallpox, mumps, rubella, polio, and a host of other diseases that used to kill a good share of kids is not a bad thing, so I vaccinate for everything but then make sure my kids get a healthy dose of germs by banning hand sanitizer, allowing eating while riding the subway, and encouraging them to handle the wares at third-world street vendors. Maybe we went a bit too far when we went to the animal markets in Jakarta in the midst of the bird flu scare and purchased a pet monkey, snake, and fruit bats (which we later set free upon leaving the island of Java). At the time I didn't yet know that bats (along with pigs) were the genus of animal most implicated in zoonosis (the evolution and transmission of disease from animals to humans). But I did know that some of the strongest support for the hygiene hypothesis is the fact that rates of allergies are highest in the most developed nations and lowest in the poorest countries, where there is a greater disease burden. Meanwhile, the flora naturally found in the guts of children is more diverse in poor areas of the world.[4]

No allergies for these Malawians . . . or for this group of Indonesians (and E and Yo) . . .

Even in the West, kids from larger families suffer from lower rates of allergies—a fact that scientists hypothesize to be related to the greater exchange of viruses and bacteria among the members. And one somewhat promising—though still highly experimental—therapy for treating autoimmune diseases involves infecting the patient with a parasite to divert her immunological resources away from herself. Yet another theory about the association between living among animals and low rates of allergies is that we simply get sensitized to the antigen. Allergic responses represent a disproportionate, acute response that triggers reactions ranging from itching to asthma to anaphylaxis. We go to the allergist to slowly build up a more "rational" immune response to the allergen through a slow process of desensitization. It might be the case that living with pet dander and the like actually does the job of the allergist's weekly shots.

Besides, pets are at the root of Western civilization. I don't mean that given enough time a hundred monkeys would have written Shakespeare's oeuvre; I am talking about the important role that living with other mammals (and their diseases) has played in Europeans' domination of the world in recent history. Namely, Eurasia enjoyed a plethora of large, domesticatable work animals found nowhere else in the world:[5] horses and camels for transportation; cows and oxen as draft animals; dogs[6] as shepherds (not to mention the sheep themselves); even my slothful, self-entitled cats served a working purpose: to keep rodents out of the granary. And that's just the working mammals. Besides providing labor, the pathogen exchange that resulted from living in close contact with these other species led to immunity from a range of diseases. This is perhaps best illustrated by two diseases: smallpox and malaria.

The vaccine for smallpox was developed by Edward Jenner when he extrapolated from the fact that milkmaids didn't get smallpox. Others had already observed their immunity due to their exposure to cowpox, a much less virulent disease. So Jenner experimented on the eight-year-old son of his gardener by injecting him with pus from an infected cow named Blossom. (So much for eighteenth-century human-subjects review boards.) He then exposed the kid to smallpox variolation[7] (injection in a limited, controlled way of a pathogen) and later to the disease itself. Little James proved robust to these immunological challenges. So though horses were said to be the source of smallpox, cows provided the cure. And of course, today, many modern vaccines are developed in chicken eggs.

Likewise, the *Plasmodium vivax* strain of malaria in Asia is a lot less deadly than its *Plasmodium falciparum* counterpart in Africa thanks to oxen. As in the case of cowpox, the coevolution of the parasite in both humans and cattle most likely led to it being less virulent than its human-specific strain. Second, the mosquito vectors that carry *vivax* are more likely to bite an ox (or cow) than a human. Thus the chances of the disease being transmitted from a human to a human are much lower since the blood that a bitten individual gets is more likely to have been from a bovine

The zoonosis that doesn't kill us makes us stronger (or at least keeps our immune systems busy enough not to attack ourselves). *Left:* One of the more exotic of E's and Yo's pets acquired in Indonesia where we lived with Natalie's brother for a short while.[8] *Right:* Yo exercising his immune system; on another occasion during that particular visit to the zoo, he was bit by an ostrich (which he reported, proudly, didn't hurt at all).

than from an infected homo sapiens. Meanwhile, the *Anopheles gambiae* (the African mosquito vector) is almost exclusively a human biter, since there were no other animals living with the humans upon which they could feast.[9]

So the next weekend we marched back to the 23rd Street Petland Discounts and scooped up the Arab and the Wimp. At first, E complained that Yo didn't have to earn his pet with sewage duty, but in the end she went along with the plan since she wanted her pig to have company. They arrived at a compromise where the black one was entirely hers but the multiculti pig was shared, 51 percent Yo's and 49 percent E's. Soon, however, such precise allocations would be meaningless since we would be swimming in guinea pigs. We didn't know how to sex the pigs, and evidently neither did the workers at the pet shop. What we had thought were two males turned out to be an opposite sex pair. And before long we had an intergenerational village of—at its max—sixteen guinea pigs running around a corral in our house.

Allergy prevention was one thing, but this even crossed my rather flexible limits. Pig by pig I managed to reduce the numbers while managing E's emotions as she parted with her flock. Some were returned to the store. Others were donated to the New York City public school system as class pets. A big batch were brought—along with a monetary donation—to a U.S. Army wife who ran a guinea pig "sanctuary" out of her home in northern New Jersey while her husband was off defending our freedoms. We were down to four males (for sure they were guys). Death took two more, and now we live with a reasonable number of guinea pigs—the original two. The rabbit has since gone AWOL, so the menagerie is gradually going from its absurd apogee to a tractable, if still large, number of pets. I must admit, however, that my kids are never sick, and though Yo appeared to be on the road to asthma when he was little (prior to us having had any pets), he now has no problems with his airways whatsoever. Whether this is causation or mere correlation, I may never know. I do know, however, that they much prefer petting their guinea pigs to getting weekly shots from my allergist.

7

Shut the F* Up, Dad!
Discipline (or Lack Thereof)

HERE'S THE SCENE: It's a quarter to eight in the morning on a Monday. I've just inserted a chewable calcium tablet into my eleven-year-old son's sleep-encrusted mouth as if I were dropping a quarter into an arcade game. Now I'm crouched at the foot of his bed. Yo has always had lots of trouble falling asleep; the result is that getting up in the morning was never an easy task.

"Stop, you goddamn pedophile!" He screams at me as I try to slip his left foot into some clean socks after having peeled back the ones he's most likely been wearing for three days. Luckily he's still in an early enough stage of puberty that he doesn't smell much at all, even when going almost a week between showers.

"Stop!" he yells again. At least he's fully awake now.

"Good morning, sweetheart," I say with an artificially saccharine tone in my voice as I tilt last night's glass of bedside water to his cracked lips and he dutifully parts his braces-encrusted teeth, allowing me to pour a tablespoon or so of liquid into his mouth as if I were a mama bird. Then I slip a purple dinosaur vitamin into his curled-up hand as if we are doing a drug deal on the streets. But I've spilled water on his bare chest and he's instantly cursing again.

E walks into his room, looking for her basketball sneakers since she evidently has P.E. today. "Out of my room, bee-yotch," he yells at this invasive species.

"Aren't you going to punish him?" she asks—or, rather, demands. Before I can respond, she has answered herself: "Of course not. He calls me ugly, he calls me the b-word, and you don't do anything. You're pathetic."

"But I agree with him," I say, "you're a B-eautiful, I-ntelligent, T-eenaged, C-ool, H-omegirl." Besides, I rationalize silently to myself, I let him get away with more shit in the morning because I figure it must be pretty hard to wake up if you're aged eleven and going to sleep at midnight.

She rolls her eyes and stomps her left foot as has been her habit whenever she's pissed since the age of one, when she could first stand on two feet. "Besides, you're just as insulting to him," I add. "You're just a lot more subtle about it."

"Oh yeah, like how?"

I stammer to come up with an example. But I can't. The

other students in her class are amazed that E has never said a swear word (even while Yo teaches *me* new curse words). At their school, the other kids maintain a betting pool as to who can make her utter a four-letter word first. And, understandably, they wonder how these two kids could be brother and sister reared in the same household. The sixth-grade boy who brought a flask of water to school and pretended it was booze and the girl who was the only one in the seventh grade to argue that it was wrong for us to kill Osama bin Laden because killing is *always* wrong. The boy who found a kazoo, a spent lighter, and leaves in the playground and, with an older boy, decided they would smoke it in the corner of the yard. The girl who argued for tree rights (yes, going beyond animal rights) and the boy who, when everyone else's jaw dropped as they saw me angrily approaching said sixth grader holding aforementioned kazoo to his lips, didn't flinch. The girl who once again found herself the lone debater on the side of the Royalists when they were discussing the Boston Tea Party and the boy who yelled at his father when he smacked the leaves and lighter out of his grip, "Dad, damn it, look what you've done now! You've ruined my pot!"

It's enough to make one think what you do as a parent makes no difference. But then if it's all genetic, that wouldn't explain their differences either. No, as suspicious as I am of birth order as an explanation, I do know that I am much tougher on E, though I would never admit it to her face. Maybe because I'm the first-born myself and feel guilty for how I bullied my sister during our own childhood. Or maybe it's all the kids' own doing, as some researchers claim: the younger one knows that they will always be behind the older one developmentally, so they specialize, instead, in mischief as a means to get attention. What I do know—from my own earlier research—is that in terms of ultimate socioeconomic success, birth order has no effect in the United States in two-kid families. For every conscientious firstborn who ends up as a chief financial officer, there's a gregarious second-born who ends up as the chief marketing officer. For every successful firstborn doctor, there's a second-born lawyer who grew up learning to argue his case against someone who was at a higher grade level. For every firstborn investment banker, there's a second-born techie entrepreneur. In an economy as rich and diverse as our own, there's a niche for everyone who manages to figure out the color of their so-called parachute. The rules of primogeniture don't really hold. Or, at least, that's what I tell myself in moments like this one.

"My god," I explained. "You're going to inhale toxic plastic fumes." I ignored his comment about pot, seeing that what he was smoking was clearly crumbled oak leaves from the tree that hovered over us from the other side of the chain-link fence.

Are my kids (okay, son) going to end up rude, self-entitled millennials because I let them (okay, him) curse at me? Duh, you might be thinking. Here's where I need to pull in another friend of mine for evidence. University of Pennsylvania sociologist Annette Lareau wrote a book called *Unequal Childhoods*, describing two types of parenting strategies called Concerted Cultivation and Natural Growth.

Concerted Cultivation is the quintessential middle-class, soc-
cer- and helicopter-mom approach. You overschedule your kids;
you hire tutors and enroll them in prep classes; you carefully
build well-rounded young men and women as if you were carv-
ing the statue of David from a block of marble. You form relationships with the other adult authority figures in their precious
little lives and proceed to make your opinions about how they
should do their job known to these folks. And you teach the kids
how to have relationships that are mutually respectful to nonkin
adults by "modeling" such behavior for them (rather than just
telling them what to do).

You want the l'il 'uns to feel confident and valued, so you
generally don't speak to them in the imperative. "Because I said
so" is not in the Concerted Cultivation vocabulary. You try to
the extent possible to offer choices to your kids and "empower"
them through Socratic dialogue. If you want your eight-year-old
to clean his body, you don't order him to the bathtub, you ask
him if he'd rather take a bath or a shower, structuring the choices
so that he feels some sense of "agency" while you accomplish the
goal of getting that wet-dog smell off. If this empowering approach sounds a lot like bread and circuses, false consciousness,
the opiate of the masses, manufactured consent, hegemony, or
any other Marxist-like term, that's because it is. Bobo parents
don't actually want their kids to have control as if they were un-
schooled hippies. They just strive for the appearance of choice:
Coke or Pepsi?

Meanwhile, Natural Growth is the childrearing model of

choice for lower-class parents and, perhaps, the French. Here kids are viewed as robust dandelions that will sprout up just fine without much horticultural effort on the part of parents. That's what our taxes are for, after all: to hire professionals whose job it is to teach our kids at school. Natural Growth parents don't interfere with teachers or other authority figures—perhaps because they don't feel entitled or confident enough to (or have more pressing things to do). And perhaps out of choice (if French), perhaps due to financial limitations, these free-range children are not over-scheduled. In fact, their schedules show vast expanses of empty time slots during which they are left to run feral with other children and learn to cope with the cold harsh world (think *Lord of the Flies*).

Theirs is a separate world from the adult world. When they do encounter adults, it's likely to be their extended kin, not coaches and tutors, and they learn to follow the dicta of these adults and speak only when spoken to. A premium is placed on obedience. And otherwise there is a force field between the children's social world (where they learn to work things out themselves) and that of their parents.

My approach basically takes the middle-class, Concerted Cultivation approach and mixes it with what I'll call "Italian fatherhood." It's a well-known fact that American men relate to their fathers perhaps worse than any other nationality with the possible exception of Germans. (Actually, we're probably even worse than Germans since they are generally awkward and stilted with *everyone*, not just their dads.) Italian men, on the other hand, are very affectionate with their fathers and sons. They hug and kiss them often. They rub their heads with their knuckles to tussle their hair. (When we Americans try that, it's called a "noogie" and is often too rough.) And, most important, they are generally open and talk about things more consequential than gas mileage, bills, or how dismally the Giants performed in their last game.

Yes, I know that it's anathema for a professional sociologist to make claims about national cultures. But keep in mind that I'm not saying there's anything innate about Italians. You take an Italian and raise them here, and they'll be just as clueless with their fathers as a born-and-bred American is. There's something about the Italian social structure that tends to produce that kind of family life. Perhaps it's the lax version of Catholicism they follow. Contrast them to the Irish—who are perhaps more foul-mouthed (and Catholic) but who still have difficult relationships with their dads. So maybe it's the Mediterranean clime. Or the fact that until recently (1872 to be exact) Italy didn't even exist but was mushed together by Garibaldi out of a bunch of small, tribal city-states. Or maybe it's all that talking with the hands. It's not important. What's key for this story is that in addition to talking about real issues (with lots of gesticulating, of course) and expressing lots of affection (physically), Italian men are constantly ribbing each other. And father-son dyads are no exception.

"*Bischero!*" my friend Egisto calls his father (meaning "moron") when he makes a wrong turn in the suburbs of Milan. "*Ma dove vai, coglione?*" ("But where are you going, idiot?") Though it does sound nicer in Italian, I don't think "moron" is a phrase I could imagine ever uttering to my own New England father despite his own foul-mouthed, Irish tendencies.

"*Vaffanculo*" (Go fuck yourself), Ettore replies to his son, with affection in his voice. "*Vado in tuo culo!*" ("I'm going up your butt!" We'll just leave that response unanalyzed for now—or perhaps forever.)

When we have our own kids, we generally either reproduce our own parental relationships or completely disidentify with them. I did the latter when it came to my own troupe of little baboons. I kiss and hug them all the time even though I am not generally a touchy-feely kind of guy. I let Yo curse me, as you've seen. And sometimes I use profanities with them—though not usually directed at them. I affectionately call them retarded (to the horror of my own mother). And I give them noogies somewhere in between the Italian and American versions—depending on my mood and how they've been behaving.

And I let them see, watch, or listen to pretty much anything they want. (Of course they must have earned the screen time.) No matter how adult it is in form or content. This is perhaps the most shocking practice to the typical, Puritan-infused American parent. However, the best protection for kids from veering off the righteous path is not the Bush doctrine of lying about "not" having tried drugs. It is openness, and Talmudic-like discussion of *everything*. Think wine in France. Kids there are taught to drink responsibly from a young age (i.e. wine with dinner), and as a consequence there are far fewer alcohol-associated problems among teens and young adults—or adults, period, for that matter. The same is true for sex. According to sociologist Amy Schalet, the Dutch allow their kids' love interests to sleep over. They also discuss the birds and the bees with their children, and consequently have a much lower rate of STDs, abortions, and teen births. Even in America, we know that it is the Bible-thumping states that have the highest rates of out-of-wedlock childbearing, the youngest age at first intercourse, and the greatest likelihood of divorce. Hypocrisy is generally bad policy. And remember, they will learn it from someone if not from you. What's less cool than something your parents do and also talk to you about?

Besides, researchers from the University of Kansas and the University of Alaska (two of the reddest states in the nation) have found that among middle-class families (and even working-class ones), encouragement far outpaces prohibition when parents speak to their kids. Only among the welfare poor did prohibitions (i.e. negative dicta like "Don't do that!") exceed positive comments. So my kids can watch whatever they like as long as we discuss it during or afterwards. Further, I will provide the definition of any word or phrase in a dictionary or urban dictionary, even such terms as "fellatio" or "cunnilingus."

I also take them to adult cinema, ranging from Truffaut's French New Wave classic *The 400 Blows* (which is actually about a kid) to the violent Israeli anti-war movie *Waltzing with Bashir* (where all the old Jewish ladies screamed at us for having kids there—I personally think they were just upset with the anti-Zionist message of the film) to the Werner Herzog documentary about a man who gets eaten by bears (*Grizzly Man*) to which we brought along my nephew, Dante, by accident.

"What happens to the main character?" my sister repeated in disbelief at her front door as we dropped him off after his bedtime—a fact for which we were already in enough trouble thanks to her adherence to strict bath, book, and bed times.

I tried to explain that we didn't know the movie was going to end that way.

"Thanks for a week of nightmares!" She said as she closed the door in my face.

Indeed, Dante did suffer from interrupted sleep those next few days, while Yo laughed about what an idiot the ursine-eaten guy was and E said we should be more upset for the multiple bears that got shot in the film than we should be for a guy who gets eaten. "He was probably threatening their habitat," she rationalized. "And grizzlies need to eat to survive, too."

All this libertarian libertinism, however, stays in private. At home my kids can challenge me; they can call me an a-hole. They can argue their case as to why they should be able to watch the latest episode of *Glee* or *Family Guy* before they start their homework or extra math. But when we are out and about—that's an entirely different story. Not only is there a list of verboten words when they interact with their cousins Dante and Diego (such as marijuana, vivisection, and anal), they are required to act slightly civilized all around. Only slightly civilized to me, that is. They are expected to be 100 percent polite to others. There's nothing more important to me than behaving extremely civilly to folks one interacts with in the agora. I couldn't care less if my kids argue with the authority figures in their lives, such as their teachers or principal. In fact, I encourage arguing, assuming they do it in an appropriately polite manner. But when it comes to civil society—interacting with their friends' parents, ticket collectors, waiters, pedestrians, meter maids, lawyers, and the entire public, they need to be on their absolute best church-lady behavior. Okay, they can argue with lawyers and bankers.

When I was dean at NYU, I learned a little tip from my boss when it came to interviewing job candidates. Academic interviews typically last a couple days and are more akin to rushing a fraternity or sorority than they are to the typical entry-level interview process at most firms. The candidate not only gives a public lecture and meets one-on-one with the faculty members and graduate students in the department; she has to eat several meals with her interlocutors and may even be invited to go out drinking or to the theater or some other event if the department is rolling out the red carpet for an academic bigwig. The folks coordinating her schedule and shuttling her between the various offices for this breakneck itinerary of meetings are usually administrative staff or work-study students. Assuming the candidate passes the other tests, these administrative assistants are the ones to debrief in order to assess the "true" personality and collegiality of the interviewee. To put it bluntly, I want to find out if the professor "kisses up and shits down." If she has the least bit of sense, she is of course going to be on her best behavior with me. I'm the dean for heaven's sake—even if I come to work in a V-neck

T-shirt and ratty blue jeans. It's the folks who "don't matter"—the nonfaculty workers who process her travel reimbursements and make sure the hotel and dinner reservations are made—that get to see the real side of the candidate. And to whom she may show her true colors.

So, I want my kids to grow up appreciating the incredibly privileged lives they get to lead—whether they end up fencing for the Ivy League or a junior college. They must say please and thank you. I make them look the homeless panhandlers in the eye and say hello when we pass them on our block. And if they ever interview for a professorship, they have to send a thank-you email to the secretary who arranged the entire visit—and not merely to help their chances of getting the job.

But as for me? I'm their verbal punching bag, their stress release valve. In short, their wimpy, pocket-protector, Parentologist nerd dad. Under this hybrid philosophy, they not only learn how to argue comfortably with authority figures, they also learn about the difference between the public and private spheres. They don't suffer the ill effects of the American "cult of self-esteem" thanks to being called retarded every so often. And as a bonus, they start to learn the map of the American social class hierarchy and the reality behind the fiction we perpetuate that, in fact, we are a classless society.

This Lake Wobegon cult of self-esteem is worth a few words. One area where I agree with the Asian and French parenting models has to do with praise. When my kids were in special education, I was careful to tell them that they were only enrolled there because we wanted the better class size, not because they, themselves, were somehow inferior academically. But then they realized that they must have been on the special ed side of the integrated classroom, since they were among the handful of kids who were pulled out for one-on-one tutelage. So, by way of addendum, we explained that we liked to get all sorts of additional help for them and that extra tutelage couldn't hurt and that we didn't understand why all parents weren't like us. To make ourselves believable we'd add, "Besides, you [E] needed help with your articulation, and your brother needs OT [occupational therapy] for his handwriting." Neither speech nor occupational therapy seemed all that stigmatizing. So we left it at that, not mentioning that each of them was behind grade level on some core academic subjects.

So, there is a time and a place for treading lightly. But once they started scoring in the high 90s percentile-wise on their academic tests, I felt free to revert to true Italian form, calling them out on occasions when they did something stupid. It was, I thought, the very act of calling them idiots that reaffirmed that I had no need to walk on eggshells in this domain—that is, I fully respected their intelligence and expected them to be confident enough in their intellectual abilities to be able to stand a few sarcastic jabs on occasion. (Though I must admit that one of Natalie's criticisms of me was that I failed to provide the kids with enough positive reinforcement—i.e. specific useful praise that they could "scaffold" off.) Further, when they sucked at something—like E did in fencing (so much for our athletic college scholarship dreams)—I didn't try to sugarcoat it. "I was the worst in the tournament!" she whined at the end of one particular week of fencing camp.

"Yes," I agreed, "you were. But there's always somebody worse than you somewhere. Just as there is always someone better than you in anything you do." So much for the *We're number one!* mentality. I explained that I was not even close to the smartest kid in my fifth-grade public school class—far from it. But, I would add, life is a marathon. One of the smartest kids, I told them, with their rapt attention, was now unemployed and in dire straits. Noncognitive skills strike again.

One of my favorite memories of E is when we were returning from a kids' track meet for which their mother had signed them up. E had placed near the bottom of the pack, but as befits the contemporary cultural trends, nonetheless received a ribbon marked "Participant." On the subway home, she said she was disgusted by this citation and tried to shred it with her teeth, eventually throwing it on the subway floor to grind with her heel as she found its artificial, rayon-like cloth indestructible. "I wish they didn't give us these. It's worse than nothing. It's like a slap in the face!"

Yo, meanwhile, had found a black Sharpie marker on the dirty subway platform and was busy crossing out "Participant," writing in its stead "3rd Place." "But you didn't come in third!" his big sister exclaimed. He actually came in fifth.

"Yes, I did," he stuttered. "I tripped, so I would have come in third if I hadn't fallen. And, and . . ."—he sucked the excitement-induced saliva back into his mouth—"another person was really too old to be in my division. He told me so." I wasn't sure whether to be proud of the entrepreneurial ingenuity inherent in his refashioning of the ribbon with a found graffiti marker or to be horrified at his willful manipulation of the truth. Or both. I decided to defer judgment to an unspecified future date. After all, while honesty is all well and great, experiments have shown that depressed people are more likely to rate their performance accurately while "healthy" individuals overestimate how well they perform.

One evening I realized that I had to step up the manners training a notch. I had invited a new friend and his family over to dinner during their visit to New York City. Matt Isler was a full colonel in the U.S. Air Force while still in his thirties. He had also been the youngest squadron commander (at the time) and was about to rotate to a desk job in the Pentagon, much to his chagrin, in order to check off that box on his résumé. He didn't look like a fighter pilot; he looked like an actor who played a fighter pilot in Hollywood. We had met at a "young leaders" forum—the kind of boondoggle that is meant to introduce future elites to each other. It's the kind of program that conspiracy theorists would go apeshit over—with good reason—if they knew about it.[1]

I immediately formed a bro-crush on Colonel Matt as he made his presentation to our group of Chinese and American jet-setters, explaining his time in Iraq as an aide to General Lloyd Austin, during which time he planned air support for the Iraqi

Army units that were sweeping out Sadr City, Mosul, and other insurgent-heavy communities, as well as helping to plan the 2009 provincial elections. So after our time in Seattle, we stayed in touch, and when he announced that he would be in New York City for the holidays with his family, I took a chance and invited them to dinner. When they stepped off the elevator in our industrial building (built just before the crash in 1929) and onto our floor, which was still zoned as a commercial fur factory, Natalie and I were stunned. Before we could even direct them under the exposed pipes and around the stacked drums of polyurethane in the gray-painted cement hallway, Matt's son thrust out his hand to Natalie.

"Hello, my name is Jake," he said in a voice as firm as his grip on her hand. "It's a pleasure to meet you, ma'am." He held his chin up and made intense eye contact while reciting this script.

His sister, meanwhile, introduced herself to me, and then the kids switched. Our kids were nowhere to be seen during this exchange. I had already been nervous enough about this cross-cultural exposure. It was one thing for me to interact with Matt in a semiprofessional context, but to bring him to my home? How would I explain the smell of E's guinea pigs or, for that matter, any of Natalie's conceptual art projects—such as the goose translator, the electronic bird perches, or the half-life ratio that tracked the value of sperm and ova in the donor economy? And how could I get Yo to sit down for an entire meal?

After I met Matt's kids and wife, I grabbed E and Yo and

cattle-prodded them forward to introduce themselves. They seemed confused as to what I was asking them to do but stumbled through the exchange of names they had grown accustomed to:

"Hi, my name is E," said the elder.

"Eve?" a confused Mrs. Isler asked.

"No, E, like the letter." She coughed. "I can choose what it stands for, but right now I like it just as E, the letter."

"How interesting," Mrs. Isler politely offered, as had many a confused adult before her.

"I'm Yo," E's brother added. By now, after his sister's explanation, he didn't have to elaborate that it was Yo with a Y and not Joe with a J, as many people assumed they had heard.

Rather than leaving Yo hanging out there, I jumped in, "After you name your first kid 'E' the pressure is really on. It's 'Yo' as in 'I' in Spanish; actually he has eight given names—sung to the tune of 'John Jacob Jingleheimer Schmidt.'"

Now Yo himself took over. "Yo Xing Heyno Augustus Eisner Alexander Weiser Knuckles Jeremijenko-Conley." He was beaming.

"Cool," Jake added, only slightly uncomfortably. And before we knew it, they were off in his room playing with BB rifles and Nerf guns. But allowing them to stay there too long would have meant that we were following the lower-class approach to parenting and not exposing our kids to the world of nonkin adults. So when the takeout arrived (unlike most Parentologists, Natalie and I are both lame at household tasks such as preparing food) we called the boys back to the table for dinner.

During the meal, we talked about the role of security and

policing in economic development, how to fly a jet plane over water when instruments fail, Natalie's idea of creating wetlands airstrips for private planes, and the drinking rituals at military bars. Matt gave Yo the "coin" for his unit and presented me with Jeremiah Weed Sweet Tea flavored vodka and some sort of concentrated lemonade, which, evidently, when mixed together become one of the quintessential Air Force cocktails. A few days after they left, we received thank you cards from the kids. Shoot, I still haven't thanked my sister for last year's Christmas present. But still, to my own kids I rubbed in how polite our guests had been.

Really, though, that was just the warm-up. A few weeks later, I was to host a dinner for the former prime minister of New Zealand, whose husband was a visiting sociologist at NYU while she took a new job as director of the United Nations Development Program (UNDP). I had promised the couple a "real New York experience," since I figured they had never been in a commercial loft before—or at least not in our Penn Station neighborhood that boasted the highest density of homeless people in the city (if not the nation), thanks to the equally abundant methadone clinics and SRO hotels. In preparation, I looked her up on Wikipedia and discovered that she had been among the longest-serving democratically elected female heads of state in the world. Great role model for E, I thought.

Every so often over the intervening period, we practiced introductions as if we were in the military. "Pleased to meet you, ma'am," I said, asking Yo or E to imitate me aping Colonel Isler's kids. "My name is . . ." We indeed had to practice, since Yo had a tendency to crack up laughing whenever he made eye contact with anyone. I just hoped he'd be able to keep a straight face on the big night. Even though it wasn't really relevant, I also explained that when you meet active military personnel or veterans, you must also add "Thank you for your service"—a little ditty I learned on one of those "leadership" retreats hosted by the U.S. military.

Photo of wimpy Parentologist Dad receiving award at the Army Special Forces training grounds in North Carolina. What was the award you ask? The "bent barrel" award for worst performance at the shooting range.
Department of Defense photograph

"And," I warned him finally in a stern voice that was meant to convey military authority as if I myself were an active duty officer and not a lame Berkeley-ROTC dropout, "you will sit still at the table, ask to be excused only when we finish eating, ask questions of the guests, and um . . ." I ran out of breath and ideas and rhythm. "Okay?" I asked in my regular tone once I had inhaled again.

"Ohhh-kaaay," he responded through his own exhalation, slouching his shoulders with faux exhaustion from my pestering. Meanwhile, I imparted a quick lesson on New Zealand (which they had evidently thought was part of Australia, since we often stopped there on the way to see Natalie's family), on the difference between a presidential and a parliamentary system, on the Labour and Conservative parties (she was Labour), and on what UNDP stood for—not to mention the entire concept of economic development. It was akin to what I've done to help prep NYU's Rhodes finalists for their interviews.

Finally, the big night arrived. I placed the order for the Indian food from the restaurant that received a "B" grade from the New York City Department of Public Health (briefly downgraded to a "C" before later recovering "A" status) but which seemed to be favored by the taxi driver crowd. When the tin trays were delivered, I quickly transferred their contents into the waiting bowls as if I were a transplant surgeon with a fresh organ. I was just in time for the guests. In addition to the Thatcheresque Prime Minister and the First Gentleman of New Zealand—who seemed to be a species with which I was entirely comfortable: bearded academic type—I had invited a senior administrator at NYU and my neighbors who were Australian. My twenty-two-year-old stepdaughter, Jamba, was also attending the event since the First

Man had asked if they could bring their twenty-year-old niece who was visiting New York during her school break.

I had made sure to clear out the cans of polyurethane from the hallway for the state visit. And when the Kiwis stepped off the elevator, I gently shoved each kid forward.

"Pleased to meet you, sir—I mean, ma'am," E said to the first elected female prime minister of New Zealand. (Probably wasn't the first time she had been called "sir" given most people's unfamiliarity with female leaders.) "I'm E, like the letter."

She shook her hand and turned to the sociologist husband. Then it was Yo's turn.

"Thank you for your service," he said, as I flinched. "I'm Yo." I could tell he was really concentrating on eye contact, as if he were in a staring contest. He didn't crack up.

Yo's military faux pas turned out okay, as she assumed he meant her service to her island nation or perhaps to the world now that she was at the UN. A smile cracked her diplomatic countenance. The dinner turned out to be a success, as we gossiped about global politics and heard stories about what it was like to be the only man among the first ladies at the APEC and other such summits. He and I bonded over being married to strong women and would stay friends long after that night.

"What does a prime minister do in a typical day?" E asked—without prompting or rehearsal, I might add.

After she received her answer, Yo piped up with his question: "Who is the enemy of New Zealand?" (This was actually kind of a controversial question, since the minister had, in fact, decommissioned the "strike arm" of the New Zealand Air Force, much to the chagrin of the Aussies, who still feared the Indonesians to their immediate north.)

Toward dessert (which my kids don't normally get to have), Jamba and the niece asked if they could be excused. They had been whispering to each other at one end of the table and not participating in the conversation other than when either of them was directly asked a question. Jamba asked if she could bring the Kiwi girl with her to a party of her friends. The Kiwis looked at each other and Peter, the sociologist, announced, "Okay—as long as you make sure she gets in a taxi back to our apartment. After all, we're in loco parentis; don't want to get in trouble back home!"

I, of course, leaned over and whispered what the Latin term *in loco parentis* (in place of the parent) meant, just as I would have had he wished them fun "pulling a train" (which, in case you're interested, translates to: *trahentes train*).

As it turns out this New Zealand farm girl turned out to have really lived it up during her night out in the big city, according to Jamba. In fact, Jamba lost her at one point, failing in her role as *loco maior soror* (in place of bigger sister). We later heard that their niece made it home at some point in the wee hours of the morning. Thankfully, I knew nothing of this potential diplomatic crisis on the actual night, so was not an insomniac wreck.

"You owe me big time!" Yo announced as I tucked him into bed after the dishes had been done. "I had to put up with that stupid, boring dinner." It was way past his bedtime. "I'm charging you five dollars for my time. Or you can give me four hours of *World of Warcraft*. No!" he prattled on, as I kissed the top of his head, "You need to give me both." I said nothing, which typically the kids take as assent and a promise, hoping that he would be able to sleep in the next morning and arise in a better mood.

From the point of view of the Parentologist, it had been a "mission accomplished." They had learned a little Latin, made eye contact, and been successfully integrated into the adult conversation with nonkin (see Concerted Cultivation, discussion on page 101). The most important part was that they found out that the national leaders they see on TV (if we had had a TV, that is) are regular people like you and me (okay, not exactly like me), and that it's actually pretty boring going to all those international summits and that politics was probably not something they would want to do with their lives (but they would now have a role model if they changed their minds!).

But before I could fully demystify the elite for my kids, I would have to get them to internalize and generalize the social skills we had drilled into them for this one particular occasion. Indeed, almost a hundred years ago, the social psychologist George Herbert Mead described children's socialization process as proceeding in distinct steps: First they learn to imitate (as with games of peekaboo); then they become able to take the role of one person reacting to another in a very specific context (think playing house or state dinner); eventually they play complex games like soccer where they need to see the situation from the point of view of multiple other social actors;[2] and finally they internalize the "generalized other," seeing themselves as an object (the "me" as distinct from the "I") that is also perceived by society around them, and thereby are able to handle novel situations with tact and aplomb.

It was going to cost me a lot more than five dollars and four hours of *World of Warcraft* time, as I would soon find out, to get from game playing—which they had successfully completed with the Kiwis—to full socialization.

8

Turn Your Feral Child into a Nice American Capitalist (You Know You Want To)

SINCE 1966, there's been a dirty little, open secret about education: school funding doesn't matter much. It was in that year that James Coleman published his now eponymous report that analyzed data from more than 600,000 students and teachers. He and his colleagues found that much more important were the family backgrounds of the students themselves and the peer composition of the school. (To be fair, some aspects of school did matter, like teachers' verbal ability.) The importance of classroom composition—i.e. peer effects—was taken by liberals to rally support for busing programs to integrate public schools, since the effects were particularly dramatic for black students.

However, busing, as we now know, resulted in a violent backlash and failed to solve the problems of unequal educational opportunity in America. Meanwhile, the "Coleman Report" set the stage for a burgeoning of radical educational theory—reflected in works like *The Hidden Curriculum*; *Schooling in Capitalist America*; and Pink Floyd's "Another Brick in the Wall." They all argued variations on the same basic theme: the latent function of schooling was not to teach the three Rs but to socialize pupils into their putative places in society. School uniforms, busywork, competition, tracking, and sitting still were all geared to the real purpose of education in modern capitalism: to get us ready to play our respective socioeconomic roles in society. Rather than being some meritocratic melting pot—the Grand Central Station of equality of opportunity—classrooms were seen to be the main stage for the reinforcement of existing inequalities (i.e. the huge family background effect that Coleman found).

Radical critiques to the radical critiques claimed—with persuasive evidence—that kids didn't always go along with the plan. In fact, working-class kids were the ones most likely to resist through anti-education attitudes and behavior, and thus school often failed to socialize (i.e. brainwash) them adequately for the labor market. Most notable among this body of work was Paul Willis's *Learning to Labour*, written not surprisingly in the U.K. during the heyday of the punk rock subculture.

Funny that back then, the group rejecting school was the far left, in order to combat the indoctrination of their kids into the capitalist machine. Today the same charges are levied by those on the religious right, who form the biggest group of homeschoolers in America, resistant to the secular influences of public education. I, on the other hand, heartily approved of the brainwashing of my kids with the so-called hidden curriculum. From the moment I set foot in a primary school classroom on a prospective parent tour, I realized that this environment was not conducive to reading comprehension, 'riting, and 'rithmetic. I was going to have to take care of that at home myself. Here, I thought, my kids are going to learn how to function in normal society. They sure weren't going to get that amid the chaotic animal farm that doubled as our home.

But somehow the lesson hadn't taken for little Yo. Despite the crash course for our state dinner, the message we had sought to impart hadn't been adequately internalized, abstracted, or routinized. Or perhaps we were just struggling to tame a genetic force that was far greater than our nurturance could handle. Either way, he was still quite feral and had trouble paying attention to cues at school.

Once on the way from elementary school to the after-school program he attended at the time, he stepped out of his shoe (again, that's partly my fault for being a cheapskate and buying shoes that he could grow into for a while). The Yo-specific part was that he was so engrossed in conversation with his line buddy on the walk over that he just kept on going. When he got to the Children's Aid Society children's center, a counselor asked him, "Yo? Where's your other shoe at?" To which he pointed in the general direction of his elementary school from which they had come. One of the college-age girls who helped shepherd the kids across Greenwich Village retraced their path and, sure enough, found the footwear sitting seven blocks away on Sixth Avenue right where he'd left it as he was debating the merits of Vaporeon's water elemental form versus his fire evolution in the Pokémon universe that dominated his brain at that particular developmental stage.

As long as he was in public school, such attention issues didn't seem to matter much. He scored well on the oh-so-important statewide exams for which the teachers and school administrators were themselves graded. During class time, he generally sat at the periphery of the group atop a therapy ball and stared out to space while the teacher lectured at the kids. He didn't raise his hand all that often, but he was taking in the material despite outward appearances to the contrary. It was hard to believe that as he played with his pencil or chewed his nails and yawned, he was learning the distributive property during math lessons or following the plot of the read-aloud, but he was right there with the rest of the class. I had tested him myself plenty of times in the good old Sears family bed during the family reading hour.

"What just happened in the story?" I'd yell out of frustration because he was humming and sorting Pokémon cards while I was reading *Huckleberry Finn* to him. But no matter what else he was doing, he managed to play back to me that, for instance, Huck had just introduced himself as Tom Sawyer to Tom's Aunt Sally in the previous scene.

So each year at the first parent-teacher meeting with a given teacher, Natalie and I would explain, almost plead with the teacher to believe us when we said that despite all outward appearances, Yo was actually paying attention. But even with this warning and filter, the challenge Yo and his teachers faced was not the academics, it was the transitions between activities and the "hidden curriculum." Getting into line for lunch; cleaning up after a project; packing up at the end of the day—these were the only times when Yo's "issues" became a real problem, because he slowed down the rest of the class with his sloth-like pace and need to be reminded often to pack up or get a move on. During the rest of the time when they were actually doing lessons, he was good to go as long as he wasn't being disruptive. (He did have a tendency to blurt out jokes instead of mathematical answers.) That's the thing with the public schools: the classes were so large that all the teachers wanted to do was manage the passel. If a kid disrupted the equilibrium, that was a problem; but if he was merely quietly tuning out, heck, that made one's job easier.

Schooling in Capitalist America was failing to seep into my son. Though the teachers always put their concerns in terms of the ultimate effect such feral tendencies might have on his *own* academic development, I knew that the real reason for their concern was that his behavior made their lives more difficult. To be fair to them, evidence was that disruptive children *did* negatively impact their peers' learning of real academic skills. In one of my favorite studies of all time, titled "A Boy Named Sue," David Figlio found that when boys are given typically female names, they tend—from sixth grade onward—to display more behavioral problems. Figlio took advantage of the fact that these "Sues" were randomly assigned to classrooms to show that the addition of a disruptive child lowered the test scores of his peers. Perhaps there was "A Boy Named Yo" effect that was coming back to bite us, after all.[1]

From our point of view, we thought that perhaps a more interactive pedagogical style might help Yo focus. So I reluctantly agreed with Natalie—who had gone to the same all-girl private school in Australia for thirteen years before being thrown out in her senior year for calling the headmistress a fat cow—that we would explore private schools. (Yes, I had married a high school dropout.) My opposition to private school had been primarily out of stinginess. But there were other reasons as well. First there was my ideological commitment to public schooling as a form of cross-class socialization. (But who was I kidding? The local public school was as economically and racially segregated as any New York private school.) And second, there were no noticeable academic benefits to private school in any of the studies worth their weight in dead trees. A NYC philanthropist who wanted to push for private school vouchers as an educational solution had offered to pay the tuition for 1,300 poor students by way of a demonstration project. The response was overwhelming, so they gave out the scholarships by lottery. This was music to a social scientist's ears. By following the winners and losers of this *Waiting for Superman*–like voucher lottery, Pei Zhu and Alan Krueger (later chief of President Obama's Council of Economic Advisers) found that after a couple of years, there was no effect from private schooling and that earlier studies showing benefits to private education must have merely been reflecting unmeasured differences in the families of kids who attend those schools vis-à-vis their public school counterparts.

Even if they had found significant, lasting effects in the lottery study, such results hardly would have augured well for a major reformulation of educational policy to include private school choice. Placing 1,300 poor kids into the private school system of New York City is like the proverbial drop in the bucket. Their presence probably did not do much to alter the overall composition of the student population nor affect the decisions of the other parents. This is what economists call a partial equilibrium result—the effect when everything else is held constant. But let *all* poor kids attend private school and all hell breaks loose: The peer composition (which we know from Coleman is important) changes, and rich parents (of the cognitively high-functioning peers) are not likely to take such a radical upending of the system in stride, as we know from the case of 1970s public school busing and its fallout. So, ultimately, knowing the "general equilibrium" effect when such a policy goes to scale is hard to predict since there are so many second- and even third-order effects of a major policy change as it plays out with parents, teachers, and other players on the chess board of education.

You can see why I might have thought private school was just a waste of money. So, truth be told, the decision to apply to private school was not highly premeditated or motivated by research but was more akin to the nonscientific way that we had approached pregnancy in the first place. Rather, it was largely because of a last-minute educational snafu during E's transition to middle school that we applied at all.

What happened was that E had been dumped to the bottom of the public school queue despite achieving the best scores on the fourth-grade tests in her public elementary school's recent history. E's downgrading was the result of her travels to her mother's homeland for a family wedding that had contributed a large share of her total of twenty-three absences. Evidently, once you exceeded eight unexcused absences in that critical year, your grades and test scores didn't matter—you were persona non grata at the top middle schools thanks to Chancellor Joel Klein's no-nononsense policy.[2] This academic snafu occurred not too long after the major financial crisis of 2008 (June 2009 to be exact), so I figured that slots would be opening up in the city's pricey private schools as financiers who were wiped out switched their kids to public or left town. So I put what French sociologist Pierre Bourdieu called "social capital" into action: namely, I contacted folks I knew who were instructors at some of these schools or on the board or otherwise connected in some meaningful way.

As it turned out, that summer I received my first lesson that Wall Street paid little for its sins, since it turned out that there were not, in fact, any slots left at any of these places. Despite the topped-up enrollments, two schools where I had particularly strong connections agreed to interview my kids. The first was the Calhoun School, billed as a progressive school, on Manhattan's Upper West Side, where I had served as a guest speaker on more than one occasion and where a childhood friend taught high school biology to Manhattan's young and privileged.

While we toured the Calhoun School during our interview, Yo wandered off on his own, looking at the student art and essays that had been posted in the hallways. He was busy asking me about *Warhammer* (his then obsession, which came after Pokémon and Star Wars but before *World of Warcraft* and Apple products) instead of paying attention to what the director of admissions was saying about class size, the pedagogical philosophy, and something else I can't remember because I wasn't paying all that much attention myself. Then he had his personal one-on-one interview with her. After we got out, his mother and I asked for a debriefing (a word, I might add, that he knew at the time).

"I don't know," he said. "I guess she asked me what my favorite subject in school was."

"And you said,'science'?" I piped up hopefully.

No. He didn't say science. He said lunch.

But she had probed: Besides lunch, what else did he like?

Recess. And gym.

The admissions director was very straight-laced and thin-lipped and didn't at all get his dry sense of humor. And the interview only went downhill from there. (At least he kept his shoes on and didn't bite anyone.) She asked him what he liked to do after school. He answered, "My neighbor Spike and I"—it was a relief to me that he got the right ordering of the name and personal pronoun—"like to go trespassing on private property."

All of this was, actually, true. Our second-floor apartment

opened up onto a back alley (where our rabbit lived) that was straight out of the set of Batman's Gotham City. The alley stretched almost the entire length between avenues (probably about an eighth of a mile or so) and abutted the backs of a firehouse, a wholesale marble and stone shop, a set designer's studio, fur warehouses, the only raw pigment shop in North America, the only fencing supply store in the northeastern United States, and a variety of other interesting business establishments in our mostly commercial, wholesale district just south of Penn Station and just east of a string of flophouses, social service agencies, and alcoholics' bars. So our neighbor Spike (yes, that is his name) and Yo would climb over the various easements that stuck out from the ground-level retail levels. They set up a "fort" in the crevice between the firehouse and the building next door. They played like kids in the country played, like parents who read the *Dangerous Book for Boys* fantasize about their sons playing in our overstructured, hypercomputerized world. Yes, it may have been a bit risky. No, Yo wasn't doing extra math to earn the privilege of wandering off with his BB gun locked and loaded to play urban warfare (at least it wasn't screen-based).

So needless to say, Yo didn't get into the Calhoun School, and since he didn't get in, they also turned down E, since they "accept the whole family or not as a package deal." So I guess you could say that Natalie and I were turned down, too. The funny thing was that Yo really wanted to go to that school, but still he felt it was funny to talk about trespassing and forget to mention that he also did a Stanford math program every day, took Spanish lessons, and fenced. He was so excited about Calhoun when we exited that all he kept asking us was "Do you think we can go?" I didn't have the heart to tell him—after he had narrated how his interview went—that, no, he wouldn't be attending that school in all likelihood.

What it came down to was the fact we had failed to instill the boundary between front stage and backstage in Yo despite the tutelage that I had hoped to instill unconsciously by allowing him to call me a fat bitch in private and cautioning him to bite his tongue in public. He didn't quite comprehend what sociologist Erving Goffman had pointed out fifty years earlier (and Shakespeare four hundred years before that): "All the world's a stage / And all the men and women merely players" (*As You Like It*).

Goffman had analyzed social interaction by relying on theater as a metaphor. Public or semipublic interactions took place "front stage." There were props (think doctor's white coat and stethoscope, diplomas on the wall, magazines in the waiting room); scripts (think always having to wait for your appointment, even when you are on time; think bedside manner: "This isn't going to hurt at all . . ."); and roles (think patient, nurse, and the doctor herself). Meanwhile, we let our hair down and let it all hang out "backstage." Social order, for Goffman, critically rested on tact as its basis. We constantly worked to save face for others—not to mention for ourselves. If you see a stranger with a big booger on the end of his or her nose, you don't mention it and try not to look repulsed. But if you run across a good friend in the same circumstance, you make sure to mention it, so he can deploy his hanky before anyone else sees it, too. And we constantly calibrate our gestures, utterances, and even our posture to be in tune with those around us. That's why, we explained to this feral ten-year-old, everyone looks at the floor numbers and not at each other in the elevator, as weird as that is. Sometimes it's important to show that you are "not" paying attention to folks just as at other times (like a school tour, ahem) you are meant to show that you are indeed paying attention by doing such things as nodding assent or asking clarifying questions.

We practiced staying focused. We rehearsed questions he might ask on the next school tour. We suggested answers he might offer if asked about his current schooling experience. And then we went on the tour of the next (and last) school to which we had been granted an interview—the Little Red School House.

This downtown school was steeped in irony, even if it refused to acknowledge the potential sarcasms that abounded within its walls. It was, indeed, very Red. Whereas Calhoun boasted alumni such as the playwright Wendy Wasserstein, the book publisher Ann Godoff, and the comedian/actor Ben Stiller, Little Red's notables included the radical black feminist Angela Davis as well as the sons of the Rosenberg spies and at least one member of the Weather Underground. To boot, it is the only independent school in New York where the staff was unionized. So all in all, it sounded like a pretty progressive place. But then you get the bill. Just like other private schools in Manhattan, tuition rivals that of universities. So the kids followed a social justice curriculum among the one-percenters, hearing lectures by fellow parents such as the former supermodel Christy Burns (née Turlington), who now devotes her life to reproductive rights.

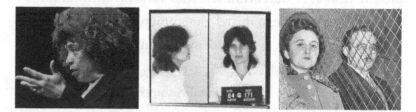

Important members of the Little Red School House progressive community then (above), from left to right: Angela Davis (*Photo by Nick Wiebe*); Kathy Boudin; Julius and Ethel Rosenberg (*Sources: Library of Congress Prints and Photographs Division. New York World-Telegram and the Sun Newspaper Photograph Collection.*); and now (*below*): Christy Burns (Turlington) (the tall one) with E to her left. E really impressed Christy, who gave her a shout-out during her speech.

Never mind that I, myself, had researched and written extensively about American poverty. I swallowed hard and escorted the kids to their interview. Or, rather, to their "trial enrollment," where they were paired up with a current student and went through the motions of an entire school day, winding up with a formal interview with the director of admissions and, as it happens, a classmate of the teacher at Calhoun I knew from childhood. (They had both gone to the "other" downtown progressive school, Friends Seminary, which itself recently broke ties with the Quakers due to the religious group's uneasiness with the income homogeneity in the student population.)

Shortly after E and Yo did their rounds, we, the parents, also met with the school leaders. Natalie showed up on her Rollerblades—as is her habit to get from meeting to meeting with the minimum of tardiness. She also carried a paper coffee cup, with her hand over it. At first, I thought that she was being extra careful not to spill her tea on the carpeted office of the director of admissions. But then, every so often I heard a chirp. Finally, I asked her to turn off her phone. "It's not my phone," she admitted, blushing. She lifted her hand as if she were a magician, and we all caught a glimpse of the injured sparrow that she had brought along in her morning tea cup. Now that the bird was out of the bag, so to speak, she must have reasoned that she might as well attend to the poor creature. So to my shock, she reached into her own cheek and pulled out a pinch of what I can only guess to have been sunflower seeds that she had chewed into a mush of sorts. "Here you go, darling," she spoke to it in baby talk as she dropped the nourishment into its hungry little beak. "Sorry," she turned to the rest of us, "I had to rescue it on the way over here."[3] The sunflower seed mash did the trick, and the bird quieted down enough for us to finish the interview. As we walked out, I figured we were going to have to homeschool our kids not only in the formal curriculum (which was fairly easy for a couple of professors) but in the hidden curriculum as well (which wasn't second nature for folks who carry injured birds around in their coffee cups).

As it turns out, our seminar on the dramaturgical theory of Erving Goffman had done the trick and both kids were offered slots at the Little Red School House. That is, by some miracle, both our kids were admitted despite (or because of) the chirping bird, and we were given the privilege of shelling out loads of tuition. So it was with great trepidation that I gave both kids the choice about where to go to school. As it turned out, we now had options: the NYC Department of Education had accepted our explanation of E's excessive lateness and granted our appeal, and she had been offered admission to the Lab School—the top-rated junior high in our district—where her two best friends were going.

Despite my own proclivity for public school, I must admit that I was a little freaked out by the Lab School; perhaps it was the flashbacks I was experiencing as I toured the school. Its building, which now also housed the "Museum School," used to be the home of the O. Henry School (aka NYC Intermediate School 70). This was the place where—from grade six through eight—I suffered almost daily neckies (where someone slaps your neck while you're drinking from the water fountain so that your teeth smash into the metal spigot); where the social studies teacher Mr. Sward was stabbed by a student (with a knife, not a sword); where the police showed up regularly; and where it was even less safe to go outside before or after school thanks to Charles Evans

Hughes High School, the 600 school that was located across the street and whose delinquent attendees used us as clay pigeons for slap-down practice after three o'clock. (600 schools were dumping grounds for "difficult" kids before the days of special education and mainstreaming. The name comes from the extra $600 per pupil that the school received for their troubles.) My heart raced as we walked to the auditorium for the principal's welcome speech during the tour: they hadn't even taken down the painting of William Sydney Porter (O. Henry's actual name). I didn't know if I could endure three years of PTSD recurrence going there for parent-teacher meetings.

Carl Sward
Social Studies, 407

Mr. Sward was stabbed with a knife. No pun.

They both chose private school. Their decision was particularly painful given what I knew about the lack of importance of school to kids' success. While a high-status or high-tuition school may provide bragging rights and friends in high places, for economic outcomes, at least, all that matters is your home environment.

How do "we" know this? Well, one study has shown that, for example, kids who get into Stanford but choose to go to their local state college because they have a sick parent to care for, or simply because they can't afford the tuition, end up just as well off economically as those who burned through $100,000 of their parents' money while living in Palo Alto or Cambridge for four years. Another research paper looked at where kids applied—as a measure of self-perceived ability—and found this was what mattered, not whether or not they attended their dream college or their safety school. (As someone who applied to Stanford and Harvard and was summarily thumped by both places, I particularly appreciate this line of research that confirms that my self-perceived ability is all that mattered anyway.) The same "non-effect" turns out to be true for high-stakes public high schools in New York City and Boston, according to economist Joshua Angrist, who compared kids who got in by the skin of their teeth and those who missed by a point or two (because these kids are basically the same, except for the somewhat random difference in their scores, which was probably due to luck). So elite schools, it turns out, are pretty good at picking winners but don't provide much value added as compared to their less elite counterparts.

You might be thinking about now: What kind of person gets into Amherst but decides to go to the University of Delaware? How can we generalize anything from them? Well, I will tell you exactly what kind of person: someone like my high school friend Eugene Ostashevsky. He arrived in New York from the Soviet Union in 1979 when Premier Brezhnev decided to let out a few Jews. A few years later, Eugene aced the Stuyvesant test to gain admission to the most elite public school in the nation (though we now know that it makes little difference in the end).[4]

That's not all. He then gained admission to Brown and Columbia four years after that. But instead of shipping off to the Ivy League, because his family didn't quite understand the financial aid process and failed to apply for loans, he went to SUNY Binghamton, graduating with a perfect 4.0 GPA after having gotten to spend half his time studying abroad. He then attended Stanford for a PhD in Russian Literature. And today he is once again my academic colleague—now a professor at NYU and a published author. The point is that Brown for his *undergraduate* education probably wouldn't have made a whit of difference to his trajectory, since his free[5] Stanford PhD essentially reset and elevated his résumé.

In sum, school mostly matters for socialization and parental bragging rights. What school you pick for your kids will most likely not affect their test scores, but it may socialize their personalities and what economists call noncognitive skills. And by the time they get to college, that's mostly determined. Princeton is valuable for its name, and for the social privilege and connections it imbues in its once and future alumni.

When I tried to tell Natalie all about this research, she cut me off: "Is there anything more important to spend your money on than your children's education?" I thought of answering "life insurance" or "sports car" (for the midlife crisis I was saving up to have), but I was pretty sure she was asking rhetorically. So we ended up as educational agnostics who took Pascal's Wager: Why not sacrifice thousands of dollars to the education gods just in case my fellow social scientists are wrong and private schools do actually benefit kids?

All this said, my New York City educational world was being turned upside down. In my day it was the rich kids who couldn't get into a magnet public school who went to the privates. I had gone to public school the whole way through—including college—until I got to graduate school. (And that doesn't really count since they pay *you* to go to a PhD program, so that's really more like stealing from the rich to give to, well . . . yourself.) But that was in the gritty 1970s and gelatinous 1980s. Now, with the incredible influx of wealth into Manhattan—the most unequal county in the United States—such logic had been stood on its head.

Despite having chosen Little Red himself, upon returning from his first play date in this new school, Yo remarked in a tone of defeat that in public school he had felt like one of the rich kids and now, exiting the five-story Greenwich Village brownstone of his new friend, he felt like the poorest. His comment actually assuaged some of my private school remorse. It didn't fix the guilt I felt for spending massive sums on my kids' school when I could have been using those funds to build wells in Haiti, but his feeling made me hopeful that I wasn't totally spoiling them by sending them to learn among the rich. Rather, I was giving Yo a broader sense of the vast socioeconomic differences in U.S. society, particularly if supplemented with sociological lessons at home.

And he was getting those in spades. Simultaneously to switching to private school, we moved into a gutted-out apartment we planned on renovating. And thanks to the tuition costs, we didn't have the money to rent another place to live while we worked on the apartment, so we created a temporary wall that separated us from the construction going on, just on the other side of the Sheetrock. We all slept in one queen-sized bed, surrounded by stacks of cardboard boxes that were filled with our belongings. Just as we had during Natalie's pregnancy with E, we again lived with only a hot plate, a tea kettle, a microwave, a toaster oven, and a mini fridge for a good half decade or more. We had one jerry-rigged sink for dishes and hand washing, and a bathtub behind which a stray mother cat nursed her newborn kittens. The dog slept with us, and the pet lizards were let out of their tank every week or so for some exercise among the cartons—only occasionally getting lost and hibernating in order to survive for the months that would elapse before we would find them again. Being the health-conscious Parentologists that we had become, we kept a HEPA air filter running 24/7 during the construction (it was free as a result of having lived within two miles of ground zero on 9/11), ran regular lead tests on our kids, and bought a water filter.

The point is that part of prepping your kids for success

involves not only training them for snooty private schools but also in preparing them for disaster. Really, success is being able to handle all that life throws at us, and as numerous wise individuals and fortune cookies have pointed out, especially important to long-term success is our skill at dealing with failure. So not only does the good Parentologist prepare his kids for elite educational norms and upward mobility, he must also teach them how to survive in adverse conditions. The cosmopolitan child of a Parentologist must be as comfortable sleeping in the park in a strange city on another continent as she is dining at the country club as she is getting home from across town when her wallet and phone have been stolen. Hence, living like a refugee was all part of the "master plan" to prepare my kids for anything that may come their way.

Thus, I expect my kids to know that they could dine on many of the fancy cabbage-like plants that are grown outside doorman buildings (as well as the cattails and acorns that grow naturally in Central Park, and various other feral sources of urban nourishment);[6] that there's no shame in Dumpster diving; that Thursday is major trash day in our neighborhood and thus a fantastic time to find free furniture and other durables on our curb; and that if you're going to chew your nails, you should at least swallow, since you don't want to let that good, pure protein go to waste.

And just in case another terrorist attack or global epidemic was indeed imminent, I stocked the mini fridge with Tamiflu (for avian or swine flu, though I later learned that the effectiveness of this treatment was severely questioned by researchers), iodine pills (in case of a dirty bomb or other radiologic attack), and Cipro antibiotics (in case of anthrax exposure). And on the occasions I tired of sleeping four to a bed, I inflated the "guest" bed (believe it or not, we did have a couple of houseguests during this period), which also doubled as our "escape from New York" raft if need be. We didn't have air-conditioning, and anytime someone complained, I announced that Osama bin Laden forbade his family from having air-conditioning during their exile in Khartoum, Sudan, in preparation for the harsh living that may lie ahead. If terrorists could survive without A/C, gosh darn it, we would, too.

Need to start them young to eliminate all stigma/self-consciousness about panhandling or busking in the subway in case they find themselves penniless and need to survive. Ditto for Dumpster diving. Here Yo and his mother retrieve a piece of furniture thrown out by the Cooper Union for his room.

In sum, even though we were earning more money than ever before, we had never lived a more hobo existence. We were prepared to survive the next hurricane. Or the next full-scale terrorist attack on New York that my father always warned of. Or earthquake. Or just a slow fizzle in the American standard of living. After all, most of the rest of the world sleeps in multigenerational beds. However, in terms of counteracting the private school effects on my kids, I couldn't win. Little did I know at the time that this philosophy I was espousing out of vestigial economic insecurity was actually elitist. The sociologist Shamus Khan writes that contemporary elites are cultural omnivores. Unlike (some) prior epochs when the upper classes tried to narrow their tastes to exclude the hoi polloi, today it is their very embrace of all cultural forms that distinguishes them from their lower-class counterparts. Namely, elites are more likely to like hip-hop, classical music, reggae, bluegrass, jazz, and Gregorian chants, while working-class ears are more typically attuned to only one genre. So I can rationalize that being able to appreciate refugee-style living (in addition to banquet life) is just another manifestation of omnivorousness. This cultural phenomenon is probably related to the plasticity necessary for success in today's economic and class structure.

As it turns out, while private school might not ultimately matter for test scores, it certainly seemed to make my kids conscious of standards of living and, in doing so, changed their behavior in a good way, to my surprise. Instead of becoming more entitled, the kids became more aware of how lucky they were. That is, though Yo still called me bee-yotch in private, in the public sphere (or, should I say, front stage) his behavior had improved dramatically. His newfound politesse even stretched to extended kin. At a recent Thanksgiving dinner he offered a toast of thanks for his fortune of living in a democracy with a strong rule of law and high standard of living. Even my skeptical mother remarked that taking the required turns setting the table and serving the food during lunch at Little Red was having a salutary effect on him—even if he did get to call his teachers by their first names there. So, maybe my money wasn't wasted after all. Besides, I considered it a (nontax-deductible) donation to the New York City Department of Education that we were now saving them the money (and considerable effort) they would have spent on him. And if David Figlio's peer effects study is correct, then we just did our small part to equalize the test scores between the public and private school students by moving his disruptive influence across that invisible educational boundary.

9

If It's Organic, Don't Panic— and Other Tips I Learned in Berkeley for Drugging One's Kids

IT WAS the very engaging nature of the teaching style, which had attracted us to Little Red, that ultimately led to Yo's academic challenges there. Most of class time was spent in peer-driven discussion, working on group projects, independent problem solving, and other "child-centered" learning activities. The kids were hardly ever just talked at in a lecture format. Alas, what this meant for Yo was that if he was listening with one ear while simultaneously staring at the sun glinting off a silvery ribbon stuck in a tree branch outside the window, that wasn't good enough because he was either letting down his group or losing the thread of debate between the Royalists and the Revolutionaries. And to boot, this interactive format somehow enticed Yo to be disruptive, whereas in public school he had been content to remain off in his own thoughts. Or maybe it was being the new kid among a group of students who had been together since pre-K that made him play the role of class clown. Or maybe it was simply that the public schools were legally obligated to deal with him, even if he acted like a drunk sailor at times, but a private school could euphemistically "counsel" one out—meaning expel him.

On this particular occasion, we had been summoned to the principal's office for yet another meeting regarding Yo's behavior during class discussions. When his English class was learning the Greek root *tele-* as in "far," Yo had blurted out, "Teletubbies" as an example. When, in Spanish, the teacher asked what *gordo* meant, Yo was the first with his hand up and offered the right answer—"fat"—but unfortunately added, "*Gorda como mi hermana*." ("Fat like my sister"—though I was thrilled that he had achieved gender and number agreement between the adjective and the modified noun.) And, of course, transitions were still a major challenge for the kid who needed to be reminded several times to stop what he was doing in order to pack up his bag and amble to the next class, or move on to the new assignment the rest of his peers had started.

So, here we were, yet again, having a meeting with the school psychologist, Yo's main teacher, and the middle school director (evidently they aren't called principals in the New York City private school system). They had already forced us to shell out a ton of money for a neuropsychological evaluation of the kid—which, as I had predicted, didn't tell us anything we didn't already know. (Had we still been in the public system that would have been free.) Now the psychologist was briefing these school officials about the results of his case study.

Finally, I couldn't take it anymore. "Are you trying to counsel us out?" I blurted. Renewal contracts for the next year were to be issued within a week or two, but it was already too late to apply to other places if, indeed, they were trying to get rid of us.

"No, not at all," the head of school stammered. Even if they had been intending to get rid of us, my bold gambit of putting him on the spot had worked, buying us an extra year. "We just want to make this the best possible learning environment for Yo."

I pushed the issue. "Do you think there is another school that would be better for him?" I asked. "Because I've certainly run through all the options in my mind and none of the others seem right." I had indeed. We could have tried Churchill, supposedly the Ivy League of schools for kids with learning disabilities (named after Winston Churchill, who was apocryphally said to have suffered from dyslexia).[1] But as much as Churchill boasted that its students were la crème de la dregs—i.e. really smart kids with particular learning issues—the Little Red chieftain agreed with the word on the street: those kids typically had more serious learning disabilities, and thus Yo would most likely be bored there.

"So you're stuck with us," I joked, trying to lighten the mood a bit.

The psychologist's recommendations all amounted to things

we had already tried. Checklists; routines; multiple learning modalities (i.e. visual *and* oral instructions); and a reward-based system for completing academic tasks that had been broken down into their constitutive parts (gummy bears, anyone?). But as the doctor wrapped up his laundry list, the head of school paused, put his pencil tip to his lips, and then asked the psychologist, "Have you considered a neurochemical solution?"

I was afraid this option would come up. I thought I had successfully avoided this sort of discussion by picking a PhD and not an MD to do the formal evaluation. Since PhDs can't prescribe medications, clinical psychologists generally shy away from pharmacological approaches to psychological or behavioral issues. My instinct about professional bias had been correct; nowhere in the ten-page report had medication been mentioned. But now I froze as the curly-haired psychologist betrayed me. "Yes," he nodded, also pressing his writing implement against his mouth as he spoke. "It certainly is worth seeing if he'd be responsive to a stimulant."

I thought Natalie would have gotten up and stormed out, thrown something across the room, or otherwise indicated her total rejection of the idea out of hand. But my expectations were further confounded when she expressed her openness to the possibility as well. "Of course," she added, returning to form, "we don't know what the long-term effects of giving amphetamines to a developing brain are." She turned to me. "Can you run some Medline searches to see if there are any long-term studies of the kids who were given this stuff in the 1970s?" Then she waved me off. "Oh, never mind. The medical industry is so shortsighted; they never assess long-term effects."

It was true, indeed. Just as the hospital's job was to keep E alive for the period she would stay in the neonatal intensive care unit, the school's (and psychologist's) job was just to get him through eighth grade and on to the next educational institution. But *our* job was to raise him to be happy and healthy for an entire, and ideally long, lifetime. Natalie and I both tacitly subscribed to the "zero-sum," "no-pain-no-gain" view of human biology—that is, there was always a hidden cost to easy interventions like antibiotics or psychotropic medications, and conversely, that long-term improvements in health required the sacrifice of short-term comfort through, say, exercise.

Needless to say, with E's infancy in mind, we were very suspicious of a pharmacological solution to Yo's school issues. So, on the way home I floated an idea: What if we gave Yo a placebo and told him and his teachers that he was being medicated for ADD?

"It's brilliant!" she said. She had been the one, after all, who had turned me on to the meta-analyses that demonstrated the placebo effect was bigger than the treatment effect in clinical trials for psychological outcomes. Namely, the improvement from baseline for the control group generally dwarfed the postexperiment difference between that placebo-fed group and the actual "treatment" group. It was a fairly consistent finding on outcomes ranging from depression and anxiety all the way through Parkinson's disease, where patients who received fake brain surgery actually presented with fewer tremors afterward.

So we put Operation Pygmalion into action. Real, old-school Pygmalion was a sculptor from Cyprus about whom Ovid wrote.[2] Meanwhile, some of the more creative social scientists in recent history, Robert Rosenthal and Lenore Jacobson, borrowed the term to encapsulate their rather stunning findings. In 1968, they published the results of an experiment in which they lied to teachers, informing them that they had developed a super-duper cognitive assessment tool that enjoyed enormous predictive powers about kids' abilities and future academic performance. The kids were randomly assigned to receive this glowing assessment, and there was, in fact, no magic test at all. But armed with the pseudo-information that certain pupils were latent geniuses, the teachers made the diagnosis a self-fulfilling prophecy by lavishing praise and additional attention on the randomly anointed nerds. They had higher expectations for these students, and they paid off: A year later the kids in the "treatment" group showed as much as a fifteen-point advantage on real IQ growth over the "untreated" kids (whereas at baseline there was no difference).[3] The results have been used to explain everything from the effects of social stigma to class differences in school achievement to the pernicious effect of racial stereotypes.

For example, psychologists Claude Steele and Joshua Aronson have shown that they can drive black students' GRE scores through the floor just by priming them with negative stereotypes before they sit for the test. (Or conversely, can improve them if they mitigate stereotype by, for example, saying the test is not a true measure of innate ability.) Meanwhile, it's not just a black thing: When white kids are placed in a room with Asians, they do worse than they would otherwise.

But what all this research boiled down to for me in that moment as a parent was that education was not immune to the placebo effect.[4] With very rare exceptions (like when I pushed back on Yo's reading), my familiarity with *Pygmalion in the Classroom* caused me to prostrate myself before my children's teachers, yes'ming them to death since I figured that a negative perception of Natalie or me could cause them to stigmatize E or Yo and, in turn, deleteriously impact their intellectual growth during that grade. But now I would stand that logic on its side—if not quite its head—by bowing and scraping and lying to them to say that we had followed their instructions.

So I informed the school that we would medicate Yo as a pilot study of sorts after the holiday break. And off I went to the local pharmacy in search of sugar pills to serve as placebos. I obviously wanted them to look like real meds in order to pull off my plan successfully. As it turns out, it would have been easier for me to score crystal meth or heroin. None of the local pharmacies knew what I was talking about; even the internet proved barren. So I switched to plan B: herbalism.

While my zero-sum, highly suspicious approach to medication applied to Western-style prescription drugs, for some reason it didn't come into play with alternative medicine. I, myself, took about a dozen supplements a day, ranging from a simple multivitamin to turmeric (to ward off Alzheimer's, since India boasted the lowest age-adjusted rate of dementia in the world) to resveratrol (apparently the key ingredient in red wine—never mind that mouse trials showed that it failed to extend life or activate protective siritins) to garlic (cardiovascular health) to co-enzyme Q10 (for muscular energy) to dandelion root (a natural diuretic to combat hypertension) to a combo of selenium, zinc, and biotin that my dermatologist recommended for hair main-tenance to acidophilus (in order to add some good germs to the others I was ingesting merely by eating off the floor) to whatever random antioxidant that was marked down on the clearance table at the Vitamin Shoppe.

I even made my kids take supplements, though I was more cautious with them. Other than chewable vitamins, I made E take liquid iron since I worried that she wasn't getting enough thanks to her vegetarianism. I also made both of them take daily spoonfuls of cod liver oil (the best thing in the world for anything ranging from heart disease prevention to cognitive development). It was the only animal product I insisted on E swallowing. At first I lied to her and claimed that it was made from the livers of fish who had died from natural causes. But she quickly realized that was nonsense. But by then, I had put my foot down sufficiently adamantly and declared the cod liver oil nonnegotiable (though I did provide citations to support my argument).[5] I also made them take chewable calcium tablets after I read that the Dutch consumed the greatest amount of dairy and have become the tallest people in the world, not to mention suffering from the lowest rate of bone fractures in old age. (Meanwhile, the Belgians next door drink beer instead of milk and suffer the consequences when they stumble out of the pub and break their hips.)

Given these tendencies toward herbal medicine, I decided that it would be best to combine the research I found online about homeopathic remedies for attention issues with my Pygmalion strategy. So I swung by the pharmacy and picked up a range of pills from extract of hawthorne berries to gingko biloba to gotu kola (whatever the heck that is). (And, as long as I was there, I picked up a massive bottle of saw palmetto in the hopes that it would act as a natural form of Propecia to preserve the rest of my hair that seemed to be falling out at an accelerating rate thanks to all this kid-induced stress.) When I got home, I put the pills into one of those weekly medication planner-dispensers. When I was done, I announced to Yo that we were going to start him on some very powerful medications.

"If you feel sick at all," I warned him with the most serious tone I could muster, "you need to let me know, and we'll lower the dosage."

I also told the school that we were starting the protocol. They offered to speak with the doctor if that would help nail down the correct diagnosis and treatment protocol. I, naturally, demurred since there was, in fact, no doctor. I checked in with Yo after a week or so. "Do you notice any difference? Are you more able to focus in school?"

"I can't really tell," he responded, picking at one of the pimples that had recently sprouted on his forehead—partly due to hormonal surges and partly due to the ridiculous Justin Bieber–style haircut that all the boys in his grade now sported that involved brushing his greasy auburn hair sideways across his face so that his entire forehead was covered with horizontal bangs. "I think," he started to say. I was getting excited. "I think I notice that my handwriting is better."

"Well, that's good, I suppose."

If not a placebo effect, the least I was hoping for was the Hawthorne Effect—so named after the Hawthorne Works light-bulb factory. The workers there were part of a study to see how productivity varied with illumination levels. The bigger effect, however, turned out to be the fact that when they were being studied, they worked more efficiently, and when they knew the study was over, they slumped. Hawthorne effects, however, are typically short-lived since, after a while, folks get used to being observed and revert to their natural pace and approach, regardless of whether the supposed experimental intervention is ongoing or not. In fact, Yo's improvement did seem to follow this trajectory.

After a month I checked back in with the school. Or, rather, they got in touch with me, since I considered no news good news and had no desire to have them ask me detailed questions about what meds we were giving him. (I had already ducked their re-quest to have some spare pills with the school nurse in case we forgot to give them to him on a given morning.)

"Can we meet again about Yo's protocol? Thanks" was all the message on my voicemail said.

It couldn't have been good news, and it wasn't. They mentioned that they had noticed an improvement in his concentration—and by extension his behavior—for the first couple weeks after break. But then he had backslid and was blurting out inappropriate remarks during class discussion. Worst of all, most of the other kids had requested not to be paired with him or to sit next to him in class. And it wasn't just his social life during instructional time that suffered. They explained that he seemed lost during recess, wandering the schoolyard as if he were an extraterrestrial visitor observing the practices of juvenile *Homo sapiens* rather than a social participant himself. This account was a far cry from the image of a confident, extroverted toddler we still held on to in our collective parental mind.

It must have been this social stigma that tugged hard enough on our strings. "Oh, okay," I stammered. "I guess we will revisit what meds he's on. We'll have to switch off Concerta and on to something else, I suppose." I had been reading about the various forms of amphetamines and related compounds that were routinely being prescribed to America's boys, so luckily was able to pull a name brand out of my head at that moment.

When we got home, I called my friend who was a psychiatrist at Bellevue and asked him if he could write a prescription for something or other in the speed family (but not Concerta, in order to cover up my lie about switching him off that drug). To my great surprise (and grudging admiration), he demurred, citing both the law and professional ethics. Instead, he referred me to the chief of the pediatric psychiatric emergency room. (I had no idea there was such a thing as little kids being rushed into mental hospitals with psychiatric emergencies. This image haunted me every time we walked past the white noise machine and into his office.)

He spent two hours interviewing Yo to determine what was going on. After all, he explained to us beforehand, attention deficits could result from any number of etiologies. Yo could be anxious and depressed and thus unable to focus on school. (Perhaps his socioeconomic anxiety had overwhelmed him in this school?) He could be developing early signs of schizophrenia, paying attention to voices in his head rather than what the teacher was saying. (He did have a fairly flat affect—i.e. emotionless expression—sometimes, which was one of the criteria.)[6] Or it could be ADHD. In the end, he brought us back into his office and sent Yo outside to wait. He told us that he did, in fact, think that Yo was a classic ADD case but that he also suffered from some mild depression and anxiety, which may or may not be related to the social problems that the ADD itself was causing. (No voices in his head, thank God.) He specifically left out the H in the ADD diagnosis, claiming that Yo did not display hyperactivity but rather evinced the opposite diagnosis—the scarily named "sluggish cognitive tempo" subtype of attention deficit disorder.

We decided to deal with the depression and anxiety through talk therapy. ADD, however, was hardly ever responsive to behavioral or therapeutic approaches (or so the psychiatrist claimed). It was, at bottom, a biochemical issue pure and simple—more than any other psychological condition. He admitted that psychopharmacologists didn't know how or why amphetamines worked the opposite way for kids with ADD than they did for "neurologically typical" adults, but they did. Something about inadequate dopamine levels in the occipital lobe.

Natalie was, of course, back to being suspicious, and asked about research that purportedly claimed that adolescence naturally rewired the brain to solve the problem by myelinating the neurons connecting the emotional center (the hippocampus) to the frontal cortex (reasoning and executive functioning) for faster delivery service and thus better decision making and impulse control. In fact, they had wanted to put me on Ritalin when I was a child but my mother refused. And I survived middle school, if barely. Of course, in today's computerized knowledge economy where we have to sit still for the rest of our lives in front of screens, where we have to know lots of stuff in order to succeed, and where there are precious few ways to make it big on physical strength, agility, and stamina (Michael Jordan excepted), it's no wonder that there's an ADHD crisis among boys. Society has shifted the ground rules under their growing feet. I had to concede that there would have been no way I would have made it through my kids' much tougher curriculum without medication. They were reading and performing *Hamlet* during sixth grade whereas I had been taking typing and sewing and reading *Flowers for Algernon* (about a mentally disabled kid who becomes a genius through some crazy experiment before slipping back into mental oblivion). They had a longer school day and fewer kids per teacher. (Going to public school at the height of the New York fiscal crisis—FORD TO CITY: DROP DEAD—meant that I had upward of forty other kids in the room with me as the teacher droned on—not to mention total chaos once we walked out of the classroom and into the yard or the streets.)

In response to Natalie's request, the doctor pressed his fingertips together seemingly in slow motion as if acting out the opposite of hyperactivity disorder. "That's true. In some cases kids outgrow ADD in adolescence," he admitted. "But other folks need medication for the rest of their lives. It varies." Immediately my mind flashed to Natalie and I, wondering if one or both of us being on meds would help our marriage. "There are some possible side effects," he went on. "I'd like to get a baseline EKG before we start, since it can affect blood pressure and heart function." That was scary stuff. "Also, there are those who think that it may cause loss of stature."

"You mean height?" Natalie asked.

"Yes," he laughed. "Not social stature. I mean height. But it's up for debate. Others think that kids on the medication experience catch-up growth when they are not on it. For that reason, lots of parents don't give it to them when they are on summer vacation and such. But as long as he's eating well, that shouldn't be necessary."

In the end, we decided that not only would we not give him the speed when he was on extended vacation from school, we would also withhold it from him on weekends. During the week I stuffed a pizza pocket, croissant, or other calorie-dense food into his hand as we rushed (still late, as usual) to school. Sometimes he acquiesced and nibbled at it. Usually, however, he claimed his meds had kicked in and that he wasn't hungry, despite my protestations that they couldn't have worked that fast. He would skip lunch for the most part, and eat only a sugary snack after school. Then he'd refuse to eat the healthy dinner of lentils or chickpeas or whatever other vegetarian fare had been prepared. And so, ten thirty at night would arrive, and the kid would probably have consumed only about 500 calories of not-very-nourishing substances over the course of the previous twenty-three hours.

"I'm hungry!" he would yell from bed, where he was listening to an audiobook or reading a graphic novel as I tried to tidy up the house. "Can I have a midnight snack, please?" I was happy that he added the "please," which was a relatively new vocabulary word when it came to speaking to family members—me, especially.

And so, I would take his order and serve him popcorn shrimp, chicken nuggets, a ham and cheese sandwich, or perhaps just a bowl of Cheerios in his bed. Part of the deal was that he had to down a glass of milk. Then he'd become a little boy again, asking me to read his *Calvin and Hobbes* book to him yet another time. His sister having long drifted off in the next room (kept company by gently squeaking guinea pigs in a three-story Manhattan skyscraper–style cage), Yo and I would lie side by side on his single mattress on the floor as the minutes ticked by, and my energy waned along with my hopes of having some evening reading time to myself. Finally, he would slip into sleep around midnight, getting a mere seven and a half hours on weeknights.

He had always slept a full hour less than his sister despite being the younger of the two—perhaps it was an evolutionary adaptation to ensure some alone time with the parents despite second-born status. (Note to self: research birth order and sleep patterns.) But on the meds he was now in dreamland for almost a full two hours less than E. I tried bringing him down each night with melatonin. (Hey, I remembered what I learned at Berkeley: if it's organic, don't panic!) But soon his neurochemistry adapted to the melatonin dosage, and he was back to his postmidnight bedtime. Finally, we figured out a formula that gained him back twenty minutes or so: We gave him 10 milligrams of the extended release version of the amphetamine salts in the morning along with 5 milligrams of the fast-acting kind. That way he was at his maximum attention during the first few hours of school and was feeling less speedy by nightfall. The only problem was that for some reason this new regimen made his eating situation even worse. Now he hardly ate a thing at all on weekdays.

My worry about his food intake led me to agree to give him whatever he wanted to eat, as long as it was calorie- and protein-rich. So while he still couldn't have soda, juice, or French fries, I plied the kid with McNuggets, Big Macs, and even the McRib sandwich (available at select stores for a limited time only).[7] On the weekends, he ate about 5,000 calories a day—more or less the same amount a typical Olympic athlete would consume while training—and yet he remained thin as a weed sprouting between the cement cracks on our block. And he slept in till noon. The cost of this catch-up sleep and eating on the weekends was not just the fact that weekend homework was even more of a struggle than before, but also that on Saturdays and Sundays he literally became a monstrous meth head coming down off his speed high.

Yo's innovative approach to cleaning up the mess he made during a meal when instructed to do so during a typical nonmedicated Sunday afternoon. Note dog on table.

It was worth it. During the work week Yo was a brand-new kid. He had transformed from a social pariah into one of the most popular kids in the school faster than he had gone from the bottom to the top of his class in English Language Arts back in his public school days. Now he was asking to stay around after school to play in the park with his friends; at night he was not playing *World of Warcraft* so much as video chatting the girls in his grade; and all this social blossoming was on top of better academic performance. He was, a lot of the time, so serious in demeanor that I worried that he was depressed. I sort of missed the out-of-control Yo who would pull his pants down at the dinner table and race around the apartment like a prepubescent Benny Hill in small shuffling steps (his feet constrained by his jeans at his ankles) as he chased the barking dog while growling himself. I wanted to scratch the veneer of this new Yo and let out the old one underneath for some air. But then I'd spend all Sunday trying to get the old, unmedicated Yo to do his math assignment that was due the following day, and I'd forget all about my nostalgia and pine for Monday when I could dose him up again.[8]

And the most amazing thing was that when I tried the adolescent equivalent of the marshmallow test on Yo while he was medicated, his discount rate dropped steeply. Not only did he do his homework first thing upon getting home, he was completely willing to wait until the weekend for computer time if it meant he earned a few additional minutes of gaming time. So it seemed that my worries about addictive behavior, delayed gratification, and possible future drug abuse had been turned inside out like an Escher drawing: it was current, prescribed drugs that were going to prevent future abuse. In fact, there's good research to suggest that those ADHD sufferers who are medicated enjoy lower rates of alcohol and drug use.

These findings are a silver lining in the newest research suggesting few long-term benefits of stimulants on the outcomes of adolescent ADD sufferers. When they looked ten years out at a treatment and control group, there were no significant differences in grades or college completion rates. Scholars attribute this to the fact that the amphetamines lose their punch as the brain and body adapt to them. Not just the positive effects go away, the negative ones—like the sleeplessness and appetite suppression—also ebb. However, by virtue of giving him the drugs inconsistently (i.e. not on any day where he didn't have a full school schedule), we were managing to avoid the diminution of their effects. Besides, maybe there were indeed long-term benefits but researchers were simply not looking at the right outcomes.

Or maybe the shortsighted medicos and economist John Maynard Keynes have got it right: in the long run we're all dead. Getting through tomorrow is what counts. We'll deal with the long-term side effects in a couple years. Now, if they could only discover an organic, herbal version of amphetamines, all would be well in my universe.[9]

10

Go Ahead and Get Divorced— Your Kids' Genes Will Never Notice

AS I MENTIONED in chapter 1, a growing body of literature now suggests that the earlier we turn back the clock in kids' development, the more profound the impact of their environment. Early childhood is critical—race and class differences in achievement are pretty much evident by the time kids reach kindergarten, for instance. Even what happens before you're born turns out to have consequences for decades afterward, as I discussed. The Chernobyl nuclear disaster lowered the IQs and graduation rates of kids who were in utero all the way over in Sweden, where some of the radioactive iodine blew. An earthquake in Chile resulted in fewer boys being born (boys are a more risky genetic bet and thus have a higher rate of miscarriage under stress)[1] and lower achievement among those whose mothers were closest to the epicenter. If pregnant women fast during Ramadan, their babies suffer. And so on. Perhaps the scariest prospect is that women are sort of like Russian nesting dolls. When a baby girl is in her mother's womb, she is developing all the eggs she will have for her entire lifetime. So not only is a pregnant woman affecting her daughter through the placental connection, she may also be affecting the outcomes of her grandchildren through effects on both the ova and the reproductive system of the developing fetus.

Not even dads get off the hook in this intergenerational drama: alcohol consumption not only results in more difficulty conceiving, but also in less healthy offspring who, themselves, have lower fertility. Meanwhile, if fathers wait too long to conceive, the risk of autism and schizophrenia in their offspring skyrockets—particularly for their sons. It turns out that in today's society not just women are saddled with a ticking biological clock.

If I were an expectant father reading this literature, I would be inconsolably panicked. But as a parent of now adolescent offspring, it actually causes me to relax. Too late now, I think, when I read that kids born in the fourth quarter of the year (i.e. October, November, or December) in the Northern Hemisphere live longer than those born in the other three quarters (when my kids were born). And I couldn't have planned the timing of our pregnancies anyway—they were arranged by that mystical trinity: Coulda, Shoulda, and Woulda. If this emphasis on early life events was not misplaced, then it was beginning to feel like my work was done. E and Yo could stay at home by themselves if I wanted to meet a friend for a drink, and I could be reasonably certain that I wouldn't return to a charred heap of embers where our house once stood. They would do their homework or they wouldn't; they would bomb Spanish (like I did) and ace biology; they both liked theater and acting despite my lectures about them not being viable career paths; and most important of all, they asked good questions.

I *hoped* it was early childhood that mattered most, because around the time they were entering puberty, Natalie and I divorced. As two hyperactive, career-oriented parents, we—or at least I—thought our marital problems had revolved around one of the main occupational hazards that plague academia, the military, and several other fields: the two-body problem. It is next to impossible for two professors to find jobs in the same city. We briefly managed to achieve it at Yale, but then, not knowing how precious and rare such an arrangement was, we squandered it.

At first we had commuted from New York City to Connecticut. But eventually, during Natalie's pregnancy with Yo, we moved to New Haven. Not only was our work demanding more of us up there and our health plan based at Yale–New Haven Hospital, but after our experience with E's premature delivery, we wanted to minimize Natalie's stress and strain while she carried Yo in utero. But once he was born (at full term), I couldn't stand living in and out of car seats and felt increasingly isolated with two young babies and a wife who worked late at the lab. So when NYU offered me a big raise and sweetened the pot with tenure,

I took the opportunity to return to my hometown, where I had lots of support in the form of family and lifelong friends. Natalie, on the other hand, stayed on at Yale, commuting to Connecticut from New York for chunks of the week.

I suppose the silver lining was my own research that showed that when moms worked outside the home, there was more gender equality among the offspring. That is, in so-called traditional families, daughters lagged behind sons. But in working-mother households, the girls achieved just as much as the boys. As a father of a daughter, this was heartening. Though I cringed when E later asked her mother to be "normal" and stay home to bake cookies.

Our commuting arrangement certainly put a strain on us— and not merely because she often had to be away at Yale for three days a week to teach in addition to whatever travel we both had for conferences, lectures, and other work projects; it also took me a good three years to accept our respective roles in our non-traditional marriage. I was the "mom" who was home with the kids, doing dishes and pediatrician appointments, and she was the 1950s "dad"—the fun one who made them laugh and did entertaining activities with them on weekends. Gender psychology aside, it felt like juggling kitchen knives and diapers.

After Yale, Natalie commuted to the University of California at San Diego for three years. Eventually, we were able to glue back together the broken eggshell of jobs and households when she got tenure at NYU as well. Being a pragmatic-minded fellow, I had figured that this final academic chess move, combined with what would be the kids' eighth move to a new apartment—one that we all could finally agree on—provided the solution to the unique stresses and strains plaguing our rocky marriage. And I had figured it all wrong. Actually, it was all the external challenges that had held us together. Like two ions with the same charge, once we were contained in the same little space rather than separated by 3,000 miles, we became unstable. Destructive behavior abounded. And the kids found themselves walking on the broken eggshells that remained from my slapdash effort to glue our lives back together.

I had vowed to stay together at least until the children were out of the house. I did this for two reasons. First, I thought that if we—or at least I—took the nuclear option off the table in our fights, perhaps conflict would not escalate to such heights. Second, I was worried about the science of divorce.

There is so much cultural heat surrounding the issue of divorce that even academic studies can get a bit singed. There are hundreds, if not thousands, of studies showing that kids from divorced families do worse on scores of outcomes. The problem with *all* of those research papers is that we can never know the counterfactual: What if those *particular* parents who divorced had actually stayed together? This is an entirely different sample of folks from the parents in the data who did in fact stay together —harkening back to Tolstoy's famous dictum. No, we must confine our inquiry to the ones who did divorce in our sliver of the quantum universe. Would their kids really be better off if they had stayed together in some other quantum state—fighting and yelling and tiptoeing around?

This non-ascertainability is magnified by the plethora of studies showing little to no impact of divorce as well as research arguing that any ill effects of divorce can all be traced to the economic circumstances of the families who divorce and the downward economic mobility of the custodial parent (usually the woman) afterward. If all it took were money to inoculate our kids against any deleterious consequences of parental choice, then I could just work harder and get out of our marriage.

But then I read a study by the cool hand of Jonathan Gruber, an MIT economist who examined changing divorce laws across the United States. He found that when states made divorce easier by instituting no-fault, just as New York did in the midst of our own split, divorce rates did in fact increase. More importantly, he showed that these kids whose parents would have stayed together if divorce had still been more difficult were worse off forty years later in terms of their educational attainment, their earnings, and the fate of their own marriages. Since he estimated these effects based on changes at the state level that had nothing to do with the characteristics of particular happy or unhappy couples, his study was the next best thing to a double-blind medical study that randomly dispensed divorce pills and placebos.

What's more, the way that divorce tended to disadvantage offspring in Gruber's study jibed with my own more qualitative research: In a 2003 book, I deployed the term "Cinderella Effect" to argue that divorce didn't have a universally good, neutral, or bad effect on offspring, but rather, its impact depended on the unique circumstances of the child. Namely, I found that the eldest female child was the most disadvantaged kid in the aftermath of a divorce because of the added, adult roles she tended to take on. While having to care for younger siblings in light of an absent parent and serve as the substitute partner of sorts to the remaining parent may be a maturing experience, it more often resulted in a child becoming resentful about having to grow up too fast and sacrifice his or her childhood autonomy for the sake of younger siblings and the family in general. Often these kids tried to escape the burdens of their family of origin quickly—the same way Cinderella did—through marriage to Prince Charming.

Indeed, Gruber found that the effect of divorce on lowering offsprings' education and earnings levels and raising their divorce rates worked through those kids' own marital history. They tended to marry earlier than they would have had their parents stayed together. Earlier marriages tend to pull individuals away from additional education they might have otherwise pursued. That, in turn, depresses earnings in the long run. What's more, as we all know, marrying younger means a higher risk of divorce.

The tricky issue is that the social world is constantly evolving so it's almost impossible for a social scientist (and worried parent) to keep up with how so-called "effects" may be changing in magnitude and perhaps even direction over time. After all, Gruber's study is now a decade old. The real kicker is that research itself can alter the very subject it studies. For example, once an economist found that, everything else equal, there was a slight uptick in the price of stocks on the New York Stock Exchange when it was sunny in Manhattan (where the trading floor is located), with a corresponding negative effect when it was cloudy or rainy in the Big Apple. Now, what did this intrepid young social scientist do? Instead of forming a new private equity fund called "Helios Capital" or "Apollo Investments" to arbitrage the finding and get filthy rich, the academic published a damn working paper about the phenomenon. The moment Wall Street found out about it, every analyst worth her salt put New York City weather into her statistical models and *POOF!* the effect was gone thanks to the wonders of data and the free market. I hope the author at least got tenure.[2]

But for me, this Heisenberg-Hawthorne-like phenomenon was a godsend: by knowing about these Cinderella and No Fault Divorce Effects and their pathways, I could actively intervene to mitigate some of the very research I authored. So all I had to do, if I understood Dr. Gruber's diagnosis correctly, was to get my kids to stay in school as long as possible and discourage them from tying the knot too early in their lives. I'd have some time to come up with a strategy on that front. In the meantime, I needed to make sure E didn't feel pressure to grow up too quickly or take on too many household responsibilities. That part was easy since I just continued to spoil my kids in all realms except math. Maybe I'd relent and let her watch *Glee* on her computer without having to walk on the treadmill during the entire episode.[3]

But the catch was that we can only counteract the social tendencies that we know about. Late at night I worried about what invisible marital fallout might damage my children in ways I could not yet imagine.

Okay, you can watch another
episode, but walk faster. . . .

Meanwhile, as E and Yo now entered adolescence, they demanded some measure of "normality" no matter how much I tried to explain that all teenagers are embarrassed by their parents—even those with moms or dads who wear suits to work and floss daily. I was wasting my breath. And, to boot, they were getting better at shaping their environment to their liking. Another emerging strand of research has demonstrated that kids' innate qualities shape the household environment much more than we'd probably feel comfortable giving them credit for. High-IQ kids, for example, manage to extract more cognitive investment from their parents in the form of, for instance, reading time. In my own research, I have even found that other things being equal, having daughters makes parents (both Dad and Mom) more politically conservative, while sons make them more liberal.

In short, I was hardly in control of anything anymore.

This became clear when, in fifth grade, Yo developed a crush on a striking girl at his school, who combined the olive skin and dark hair of her Mexican father with the bright blue eyes of her Swedish-American mother. All was going well with this budding friendship until we traveled across the sea to visit the kids' cousins in Australia on our last predivorce family vacation. The disaster struck on a balmy, antipodal summer day, which happened to be Boxing Day, the morning after Christmas. Yo had left his Facebook account logged in and visible on our laptop, and his favorite cousin, Alex, sent a message to the object of Yo's crush, saying "Yo thinks you're hot —signed his cousin, Alex, he's going to kill me."

When Yo discovered this hack, the cognitive dissonance was simply too great for him to bear. He, of course, felt betrayed and crushed by the prank. But he adored this slightly older relative like a brother and, besides, Alex was way bigger and Australians are among the sportiest folks in the world,[4] so Yo couldn't have beaten him up even if he tried. Instead, the entire extended family powwowed on how to fix the situation—because, after all, crushes had never been secrets in our household.

We tried to reassure him that at least Alex had signaled that it was he, Alex, writing rather than passing the note off as Yo's own handiwork. But nothing would soothe him as he paced back and forth, scratching the mosquito bites that speckled his pale, Northern Hemisphere skin. All communication between the girl and Yo had gone dead since the missive had gone out. We suggested writing "Yep, he's dead. I killed him" to break the tension.

He demurred, and the more time that passed, the more awkward things became. Finally, back in snowy North America, the day before school was to restart, we—he and I—collectively sent an ice-breaking Facebook message that read, "Hope you had a good break. I apologize for my rude cousin. See you at school." As it turned out, "apologize" was a very uncool word for ten-year-olds (my poor choice, alas), and she laughed more at that missive than the original message. Or so he overheard in computer class. I was thus forever banned from his Facebook account—and his social life. For revenge, he vandalized my Wikipedia page, writing that I had herpes and was famous for being the father of him.

Each day I asked him for real-life status updates. Had he talked to her? What about asking her to the school dance? "Dad," he sighed. "We don't talk to each other. Everything is done through Facebook." I asked him why he only ever wrote status updates and never messaged her directly.

"Dad!" he yelled. "You're hopeless." I would never understand, evidently. But I couldn't stop wondering how messages could be targeted to particular folks when they are publicly posted to everyone. Did they exist in some special code the way Bill Clinton wore the tie Monica gave him during a particular press conference? Was it more like Al Qaeda's secret communication via coded words on the web?

It was just the first taste of the boundaries that my kids were setting up. When the next year Yo became the first boy to have a girlfriend in the sixth grade (for all of three days, till her parents found out and put an end to it), I didn't know about it until after the fact.[5] And that would be the last thing I would ever be informed about, evidently, with respect to his romantic life. I had read some research suggesting that men's marital satisfaction hit its lowest point right around the time their teenage sons started dating. I wondered if that was because they were jealous of the freedom that their male heirs had to begin to explore the opposite sex or because it coincided with the point at which the kids shut their parents out from their worlds. Luckily by then I was legally separated, so there was no more marital satisfaction for him to drain away. Since I was just starting to date myself, I figured we'd pursue a "don't ask, don't tell" policy for the next few months—or decades, as the case may be.

The next step was that he banned me from lying on his bed at night during the time we usually read together. Now, after his midnight snack, I had to curl up at the foot of his bed like one of our cats and read to him from there. And yes, it was an actual bed, rather than a mattress on the floor. After searching in vain in the downtown Manhattan versions of the Goodwill store, I dutifully went online and ordered bedroom sets for the kids. As I pressed Submit Order on the ones they had chosen, I heard Natalie's voice somewhere in my head screaming about the off-gassing of the formaldehyde that they used to process the wood chips into the press-board furniture pieces before they covered them with a cherrywood veneer. I tried to get secondhand stuff, I argued back with her in my brain. I tried. Of course, I could have just bought them more expensive pieces made of solid wood, but I was a cheapskate after all, not to mention broke from private school tuition.

And what did he want me to read him as I huddled suppliantly at his feet on his off-gassing toxic bed?

Of all things, the Bible!

Growing up, I had known a cute girl named Juliette who had been a child-prodigy playwright, putting on a performance at Joseph Papp's famous Public Theater at age twelve. She had it in her genes, I suppose. She was the daughter of Barbara Garson, author of the 1960s antiwar classic *MacBird*, among other plays and novels. Barbara was such a darling of the left that she was nominated and ran for vice president in 1992 on the Socialist Party Ticket. Vice President Garson raised Juliette in the same Westbeth Artists' Housing that my parents moved us to after a friend of mine was shot back on the Lower East Side. According to my mother, Juliette had been raised like many Dutch adolescents are, having few restrictions.

She was quite cute, so after my divorce I inquired as to what became of her. In a possibly apocryphal account, I heard that she had rebelled in the only direction possible—rightward. According to maternal scuttlebutt, she'd become an Orthodox Jew, made Aliyah to Israel, and now raises a huge chowder of offspring in a home in which she does not allow unrelated males to set foot. So much for a date.

So perhaps it should not have come as a surprise that Yo wanted to delve into the King James Bible. I couldn't argue with reading the urtext of Western civilization, especially since I hadn't read one page of it myself. And the deeper we got into the text, the more I realized how much it must have appealed to his *World of Warcraft* sensibilities now that we had finished reading all the Greek myths.

But the Bible reading was just one sign that the kids were demanding more normalcy and autonomy. "I can come home by myself," Yo scolded me when I picked him up from his after-school activities.

"You don't need to come get me either," E concurred, much to my surprise.

At first I told myself that even if they were saying they didn't exactly need me to escort them home like a chain gang, they actually appreciated knowing that they had a Parentologist who cared enough to take time out of his day to be there smiling when they emerged from the Little Red School House. But when even E—who was the more demonstratively affectionate one—announced, "Dad, I like to walk with my friends for a bit after school, so I rather you just give us snack money in the mornings than pick us up," I got the message and stayed at my office.

There were some hiccups in this new plan; a couple times E got lost in the wilds of southern Manhattan. Luckily I had given her emergency cab money and she came home that way. Another time she got on the right subway line going the wrong direction and ended up in Brooklyn. She got hold of me, and I told her how to get back to our little island. When she got home, I showed her the video clip of the Sesame Street sequence from my childhood where a preschooler gets lost, passing a whole bunch of psychedelic, trippy creatures and structures (like a hippo on a pogo stick and a plastic diner that emits light and steam).[6] He finally runs into a yo-yo–dangling character dressed in some multicolored duds who steps out of a dimensional door to greet him (with the voice of Dizzy Gillespie) but who then, when asked to help the kid get home again, suggests that the little guy figure it out himself: "Try to remember everything you passed, but when you go back, make the first thing the last. Ha! Ha!" (My generation may be stupider than the millennials when it comes to math, science, and the classics, but is it any surprise that we are more independent?)[7]

Just don't take any candy from him or follow him to a dark alley, and you'll probably make it home okay.

At least E made it home unscathed. Yo wasn't so lucky a few weeks later. He was mugged right outside our front door as he was getting his key out. The assailant took the iPad that the school had given the seventh graders as a learning aid. When he got upstairs safely, Yo called me at the office to tell me what had happened. Luckily he wasn't hurt. We traipsed up to the Midtown South NYPD precinct, past the banner declaring it "The Busiest Precinct in the World" and into the room full of detectives, one of whom would take Yo's statement for the police report (that we needed, I might add, to prove to the school that we didn't just lose it). And despite a contemporaneously emerging scandal that the police were underreporting crimes to keep the statistics down, they took his description and inquired about the presence of tracking software on the device and/or of a security camera at the entrance to our building. Alas, neither had been installed. Yo's meds must have tapered off by then since, while the detective spoke, I noticed him wandering off to carefully study the WANTED flyers that hung in layers off the bulletin boards. But unlike when he was distracted during the Calhoun School tour, on this occasion I was glad that the police sketches and grainy security camera still images caught his eye. He seemed to be taking in a lot, and I was happy that this experience had given him a little taste of the world outside the cloistered walls of the Little Red School House—even if I knew the story would morph into some sweet sweetback's badassssss song by the time he went back to class and told his friends about it. Sure enough, before long, in Yo's telling, the assailant had threatened him with a knife after he first bravely refused to part with the school property.

The most amazing thing happened when we got home. He drifted off to sleep at eight thirty. I let his homework slide, sending an email to his teachers alerting them to the fact that he'd be late with the assignments on account of his unfortunate incident. What's more, he slept for eleven full hours without calling out "D-A-D!" in the middle of the night after a nightmare, which was a common enough occurrence.

Meanwhile, in my own work, I was skating at the intersection of genetics and social science. I had begun my career as a social scientist by studying the transmission of class from parents to children. If half of our kids' chances in life were due to their family background, the field of behavioral genetics would have us believe that the lion's share of that predictive power of family of origin is due to genetics. According to these studies, about half of the variation in incomes or job situations is due to our genetic makeup. And only about one-sixth results from the household environment, a realm in which parents might exert some conscious influence. The remaining one-third is purported to be the product of random events outside a family's control: an inspiring teacher, a traumatic accident, or a lucky break at work.

I initially went into the field of genetics to prove these researchers wrong. Genes couldn't matter that much, I figured. It just didn't jibe with what I saw around me: siblings seemed so different from each other; I knew plenty of poor kids growing up whom I could have imagined achieving great heights had they been reared in better circumstances; and, likewise, throughout my own adult life and career I had gotten to know plenty of folks who seemed to be of mediocre talent despite their fancy pedigrees, elite schooling, and ultimate economic success. Social environment had to count for more. So I decided to go right after the geneticists' core assumption.

The way that they calculated how much a given trait was due to genetics—be that extroversion or earnings—was by comparing how alike identical twins were with respect to that characteristic to how alike (same sex) fraternal twins were. The logic is that the fraternal twins share half their genes and the identical twins share all of them, so the degree to which identical twins are more alike than their fraternal counterpart pairs reflects the genetic contribution to that trait. However, this nifty little calculation relies on one hugely problematic axiom known as the "equal environments assumption." Put in English, these researchers had to take as a given the notion that identical twins are not treated any more similarly to each other than fraternal twins are (and that identical twins don't interact with each other more than fraternal twins do in ways that might affect the outcomes in question—i.e. that their mutual, reciprocal influence is no different than that of same-sex fraternals). Since in my own experience I often couldn't even tell who was who in an identical twin set, it seemed obvious to me that identical twins were experiencing much more similar environments than fraternal twins in ways that were not generalizable to us non-twins in the population, and thus the behavioral geneticists were inflating the effects of genes and correspondingly underestimating the impact of family environment.[8]

Determined to prove them wrong and save the day for social scientists, I thought of a trick that would have been unimaginable before the days of the Human Genome Project: I would take the fraction of twins who thought they were identical when they were really fraternal (and vice versa) and run the same analysis on them. If they thought they were fraternal twins their whole lives but the laboratory genetic test revealed they were actually identical, we could be sure that they weren't raised with more similar environments because they had been (mistakenly) socialized as fraternals. And ditto in reverse. But when I ran these folks through the statistical models, the results didn't refute the behavioral geneticists at all. In fact, my models confirmed the high genetic heritability for everything from height to high school GPA to—you guessed it—ADHD.

So as a social scientist, I had to admit defeat—for the time being at least.[9] But, I must confess, as a parent it provides me a bit of a relief. On the one hand, if my kids' chances in life are largely determined by the DNA that their mother and I have passed on, all my math drilling and insistence on reading may have been of little added value. But on the other hand, all the things I did to mess them up probably won't actually matter all that much in the end either. And anything I did do right that may have mattered happened when they were wee little babies (or before they were even conceived). So, either way, I could really relax now that they were both well into the double digits. After many years of parenting, I am happy to be reduced to what my biology professor called me and all men: a sperm delivery system (and, I'd like to add, an interactive bio-reader of children's books). My own personal concerns aside, these results on the strength of genetic inheritance would go a long way in explaining why we can't seem to find any effect on outcomes of what school kids attend. And it probably means that what my buddy Annette Lareau found about parenting styles—Concerted Cultivation versus Natural Growth—correlates with class status but does not cause it.

Besides, there are other unexpected benefits of this rise in genomics. Like the analysts on Wall Street who incorporated Manhattan weather into their mathematical models, once we know about our "innate" tendencies, we can do something about them. With this in mind, I subjected my entire family to genetic testing, or what Natalie calls "recreational genomics." Fun facts gleaned from the analysis of a half million loci include the fact that my mother, myself, and Yo all have a variant of the opioid receptor that makes us susceptible to being heroin addicts. ("Oy!" in my mother's words, "Another thing to worry about with him.") Yo is slightly more genetically similar to Natalie's father than any of his other grandparents—thanks to the randomness of DNA recombination—while E shares more genetic material with my mother. I have a lower nonverbal IQ than the rest of my family, but at least the kids and I share a variant of a dopamine receptor that means we are "better able to learn from our mistakes," while their mother has the risky allele—the one that is supposed to make folks keep doing naughty things for the rush that they get from them.

While the company we used to analyze our DNA didn't at first report the infamous APOE3 allele that is strongly associated with Alzheimer's, I was able to download the raw data and check myself to see if we had the problematic marker.[10] My father has it. My mother doesn't. I lucked out. But my kids were not so lucky. They each got one copy from their mother. I'm banking on the fact that there will be a treatment or prevention discovered in the next fifty or sixty years before they seriously face any risk of developing symptoms of having the disease. (My father isn't so lucky, of course.) How this information will change my parenting behavior I don't know. Genes seem to be in a different class than sunny days on Wall Street in that most folks seem to feel powerless in the face of genetic information. One study that looked at folks who tested positive for the genetic defect that leads to Huntington's disease (and all but certain death by age forty) found that these folks didn't alter their behavior at all. They lived their lives as if their expected lifespans were the same as the rest of us. It could be the well-documented optimistic bias that most of us carry around inside. Or it could be simply that we aren't very well equipped to deal with our own mortality. On the other hand, with testing for the BRCA I and II variants that raise women's risk of breast cancer, more and more women who test positive for the risky alleles are opting for radical, bilateral preventative mastectomies—including sex symbol Angelina Jolie.

As more and more information about our genetic susceptibilities emerges, individuals and families will face the choice of whether to know the risks they face. Optimistically, with knowledge comes power. Since most outcomes are what we call G by E—that is, the result of genetic and environmental factors interacting—we can alter our behavior. While I haven't started my kids on turmeric supplements to reduce their risk of Alzheimer's yet (see chapter 9), I will never let them play football or box (as I did) or pursue any other high contact sport that increases the risk of beta amyloid plaques developing in their precious brains. But other information is harder to live by: How, for example, does knowing that you are at greater genetic risk for obesity fortify you to eat a healthy, lower-calorie diet—especially when the mechanism for how some of that genetic risk manifests is by increasing appetite?

And soon enough, we may be living in a brave new world of prenatal genomic screening. Now that we can genotype fetuses merely by drawing the blood of the mother, extracting and separating offspring DNA from the mother's by comparing it with the father's, we can selectively abort kids who have a higher risk for any number of conditions from obesity to heart disease to low IQ. The dystopia of the 1990s Ethan Hawke film *Gattaca* will shortly be a viable option for some of us. In fact, at one recent genetics conference in Iceland, I met a Dutch fellow who worked for the Beijing Genomics Institute. BGI is busy trying to assemble samples of DNA from across the world, offering to sequence it for free, in order to determine the genetic loci that predict extremely high IQ. Their young European representative, whom I met at the conference, said he went into this area because he hopes to have his own kids the Gattaca way some day—by prenatally selecting the ones with the "best" genetic potential. Good luck to him landing a date!

All this genomic science aside, when I look at the heritability literature, there are still a bunch of outcomes that seem to be strongly affected by parenting—everything from civic participation to smoking to sexual initiation to preference for loud music. For example, the best single predictors of teenage cigarette use are parental smoking and the quality of the parent-child relationship. And, in one of the rare field experiments in political science, Don Green and his colleagues showed that once you induce individuals to vote one time (by randomly urging some registered voters in New Haven to go to the polls on election day and leaving other "control" voters alone), they are more likely to vote in future elections—i.e. voting is habit-forming. Presumably, this works intergenerationally as well, since parental voting is also strongly associated with an offspring's likelihood to participate in elections. And since I have taken E and Yo into the voting booth with me every election since they were old enough to stand, I can't imagine them not exercising their rights to suffrage as soon as they turn eighteen.

So while my scientific parenting may not matter for their SAT scores, it may reap benefits in terms of good citizenship and lung cancer risk (not to mention the integrity of their eardrums). Values, it would seem, are a matter of upbringing. Looking homeless people in the eye, treating people with respect out in the public square, caring about the well-being of other species, drive and commitment, attachment and peer relationships (not to mention ability to live like a refugee) are all subject to nurture. And even if all my mathematical bribery adds nothing to their standardized test scores, at least the endless hours I spent reading to them conveyed to them the subtext that I cared, which, as I said at the start, is all that matters in the end. It doesn't matter whether you tell them you love them. In the words of many an undergraduate writing instructor: Show—don't tell. Scientific parenting is my ode of parental love.

I can already see my parenting efforts play out in their personalities. To buy their participation in (and exploitation by) this book, I paid them each 6 percent of the proceeds. E said she couldn't care less about the money unless she could spend it on pets. I allowed her one additional animal in the house (an Australian marsupial sugar glider); the rest she wanted to donate to help save animals or poor people. If she has one vice, it might be pride. She wants to publish a novel before she's "over the hill" (i.e. seventeen) and has made a pretty good start. It's about a girl who hears the voices of animals and plants. Needless to say, it's a lot better than the book about elves and fool's gold that I wrote and sent to agents when I was her age. Besides, she'll have a lot better chance getting it published since winning the National Scholastic Art & Writing Awards Scholarship for her mini memoir about her parents' divorce.

Meanwhile, her just-as-driven brother became obsessed spending his 6 percent on a piece of Detroit real estate after one of his mother's students mentioned that you could buy a place for a couple thousand dollars there. He devoted hours on the real estate website Trulia.com comparing crime rates, walkability indices, and school district scores. In the process, he's learned about bigger concepts, including the fact that white residents tend to report property crimes at higher rates than African Americans do. He's also seen segregated America up close when we went to a ghetto of Philadelphia to look at a potential property after my gently steering him away from Michigan and toward a closer, if slightly more expensive, city.

Though they appear to be motivated by fundamentally different goals—pride v. profit—I am equally proud of them and recognize the underlying obsessive drive as stemming from a common root. After all, I donated some of my earnings from my childhood job sweeping the Ukrainian meeting hall to help poor Haitian kids. But the rest I invested in penny stocks when I was Yo's age—enjoying the run up of the Reagan bull market so that I had a nice chunk of change to spend by the time I got to college (luckily before the 1987 crash). Yo, while not investing in Wall Street, enjoys no shortage of money-making schemes: For example, he went to our neighborhood bank branch and traded $50 for a stack of twenty-five $2-bills and then turned around and sold them for $3 a pop to his classmates as mint-condition "rare" issues.

So next time Yo calls me bee-yotch, I know just what to say as I give him a noogie: "Fine, I'm a bitch, so you know what that makes you, you little SOB?" And I will be more than a little bit right. The apple probably doesn't fall so far, after all.

Acknowledgments

Aber, J. Lawrence. 2012. "Confirmation of Attachment Theory." New York, NY: New York University, Steinhardt School of Education.

Bakeman, Karl. 2012. "Framing Around Laboratory Experiments on Children." New York, NY: W.W. Norton & Co.

Conley, Alexandra. 2012. "Sistering and Reading of *Diary of a Wimpy Dad*: Suggested Deletions." New York, NY.

Conley, Ellen. 2012. "General Mothering and Screening for Family Embarrassment and Child Protective Services Potential Flashpoint," New York, NY.

Conrad, Ariane. 2012. "Book Doula: Free Advice." Berlin, Germany.

Duneier, Mitchell. 2012. "Title Tweak." Princeton, NJ: Princeton University, Department of Sociology.

Flora, Carlin. 2012. "General Editorial Comments." New York, NY.

Haney, Lynne. 2012. "*Diary of a Wimpy Dad*: Emphasis on Moral Values." New York, NY: New York University, Department of Sociology.

Holmes, Lauren. 2012. "*Diary of a Wimpy Dad*: General Comments." New York, NY: New York University, Faculty of Arts and Sciences.

Humphreys, Ann. 2012. "Parentology Definition, Chapter Titles, General Edits." Brooklyn, NY.

Jacquet, Jennifer. 2012. "Reading of the *Childrearing Lab Manual*." Vancouver, B.C.: University of British Columbia.

Jennings, Jennifer. 2011. "Deletion of Potentially Ruinous Digit-ratio Anecdote." New York, NY: New York University, Department of Sociology.

Jeremijenko, Natalie. 1998–2013. "Co-Parenting." New Haven, CT: Yale University; San Diego, CA: University of California; New York, NY: New York University.

Karp, Jonathan. 1998–2013. "Bidding on *Honky*. Publishing *Parentology*." New York, NY: Simon & Schuster.

Kramer, Sydelle. 2012. "Book Proposal Development, Marketing and Sale." New York, NY: Susan Rabiner Agency.

LeBlanc, Adrian Nicole. 2012. "Structural Adjustments." New York, NY.

Lobel, Judith. 2005–2011. "General Therapeutic Assistance." New York, NY.

Nakazato, Emi. 2011–2012. "Research Assistance, Editing, Framing." New York, NY.

Painton, Priscilla. 2012–2013. "Executive Editorship: Saving Me from My Worst Literary Instincts." New York, NY: Simon & Schuster.

Schneider, Naomi. 2012. "Reframing Read." Berkeley, CA: University of California Press.

Singh, Anjali. 2012. "Acquisition." New York, NY: Simon & Schuster.

Winograd, Katie. 2013. "Shtick/schtick and Other Usages." New York, NY: Russell Sage Foundation.

Sources for Additional Reading

Dairy and Height

De Beer, H. (2004). Observations on the history of Dutch physical stature from the late-Middle Ages to the present. *Economics & Human Biology, 2*(1), 45–55.

de Beer, H. (2012). Dairy products and physical stature: A systematic review and meta-analysis of controlled trials. *Economics & Human Biology, 10*(3), 299–309.

Vitamin D Deficiency in North America

Hanley, D. A., and Davison, K. S. (2005). Vitamin D insufficiency in North America. *The Journal of Nutrition, 135*(2), 332–337.

(For references on college attendance, see page 206.)

Prenatal Steroid Administration

Reassuring

Dalziel, S. R., Rea, H. H., Walker, N. K., Parag, V., Mantell, C., Rodgers, A., and Harding, J. E. (2006). Long-term effects of antenatal betamethasone on lung function: 30-year follow up of a randomised controlled trial. *Thorax, 61*(8), 678–683.

Dessens, A. B., Smolders-de Haas, H., and Koppe, J. G. (2000). Twenty-year follow-up of antenatal corticosteroid treatment. *Pediatrics, 105*(6), e77.

Worrying

Noorlander, C. W., Visser, G. H. A., Ramakers, G. M. J., Nikkels, P. G. J., and De Graan, P. N. E. (2008). Prenatal corticosteroid exposure affects hippocampal plasticity and reduces lifespan. *Developmental Neurobiology*, 68(2), 237–246.

Long Shadow of Prenatal Conditions

Conley, D., and Bennett, N. G. (2000). Is biology destiny? Birth weight and life chances. *American Sociological Review*, 65, 458–467.

Conley, Dalton, Strully, Kate, and Bennett, Neil G. (2003). *The Starting Gate: Birth Weight and Life Chances.* Berkeley, CA: University of California Press.

Almond, D., Mazumder, B. The effects of maternal fasting during Ramadan on birth and adult outcomes. 2008. Cambridge, MA: NBER Working Paper No. 14428.

Doblhammer, Gabriele and Vaupel, James W. (2001). Lifespan depends on month of birth. *PNAS* vol. 98, no. 5: 2934–2939.

van Ewijk, Reyn. (2011). Long-term health effects on the next generation of Ramadan fasting during pregnancy. *Journal of Health Economics* 30, Issue 6: 1246–1260.

Almond, Douglas, Edlund, Lena and Palme, Mårten. (2009). Chernobyl's Subclinical Legacy: Prenatal Exposure to Radioactive Fallout and School Outcomes in Sweden. *Quarterly Journal of Economics.* 124, 4: 1729–1772.

Birth Cohort Size

Berger, M. C. (1985). The effect of cohort size on earnings growth: a reexamination of the evidence. *The Journal of Political Economy*, 93(3), 561–573.

Hierarchy and Stress Response

Sapolsky, R. M. (1990). Stress in the wild. *Scientific American*, *262*(1), 116–123.

Sapolsky, R. M. (2004). *Why Zebras Don't Get Ulcers: The Acclaimed Guide to Stress, Stress-Related Diseases, and Coping—Now Revised and Updated.* Holt Paperbacks.

Sapolsky, R. M. (2005). The influence of social hierarchy on primate health. *Science*, *308*(5722), 648–652.

Stress Eating

Adam, T. C., and Epel, E. S. (2007). Stress, eating and the reward system. *Physiology & Behavior*, *91*(4), 449–458.

Inflammation and Chronic Disease

Crimmins, E. M., and Finch, C. E. (2006). Infection, inflammation, height, and longevity. *Proceedings of the National Academy of Sciences of the United States of America*, *103*(2), 498–503.

Prenatal Stress in Mice/Rats

Buitelaar, J. K., Huizink, A. C., Mulder, E. J., de Medina, P. G. R., and Visser, G. H. (2003). Prenatal stress and cognitive development and temperament in infants. *Neurobiology of Aging*, *24*, S53–S60.

Lemaire, V., Koehl, M., Le Moal, M., and Abrous, D. N. (2000). Prenatal stress produces learning deficits associated with an inhibition of neurogenesis in the hippocampus. *Proceedings of the National Academy of Sciences*, *97*(20), 11032–11037.

Weinstock, M. (2008). The long-term behavioural consequences of prenatal stress. *Neuroscience & Biobehavioral Reviews*, *32*(6), 1073–1086.

Post-Natal Bonding Counteracts Effects

Vallée, M., Mayo, W., Dellu, F., Le Moal, M., Simon, H., and Maccari, S. (1997). Prenatal stress induces high anxiety and postnatal handling induces low anxiety in adult offspring: correlation with stress-induced corticosterone secretion. *The Journal of Neuroscience*, *17*(7), 2626–2636.

Vallée, M., Maccari, S., Dellu, F., Simon, H., Le Moal, M., and Mayo, W. (2008). Long-term effects of prenatal stress and postnatal handling on age-related glucocorticoid secretion and cognitive performance: a longitudinal study in the rat. *European Journal of Neuroscience*, *11*(8), 2906–2916.

Lemaire, V., Lamarque, S., Le Moal, M., Piazza, P. V., and Abrous, D. N. (2006). Postnatal stimulation of the pups counteracts prenatal stress-induced deficits in hippocampal neurogenesis. *Biological Psychiatry*, *59*(9), 786–792.

Stressed Mice Do Better When Test Conditions are Stressful

Champagne, D. L., et al. (2008). Maternal care and hippocampal plasticity: evidence for experience-dependent structural plasticity, altered synaptic functioning, and differential responsiveness to glucocorticoids and stress. *The Journal of Neuroscience*, *28*(23), 6037–6045.

Perry Preschool Reanalysis

Heckman, J. J., Moon, S. H., Pinto, R., Savelyev, P. A., and Yavitz, A. (2010). The rate of return to the High Scope Perry Preschool Program. *Journal of Public Economics*, *94*(1), 114–128.

Cunha, F., Heckman, J. J., and Schennach, S. M. (2010). Estimating the technology of cognitive and noncognitive skill formation. *Econometrica*, *78*(3), 883–931.

Attachment Theory

Ainsworth, M. D. S., Blehar, M. C., Waters, E., and Wall, S. (1979). *Patterns of Attachment: A Psychological Study of the Strange Situation.* Lawrence Erlbaum.

Main, Mary, and Solomon, Judith (1990). "Procedures for Identifying Infants as Disorganized/Disoriented during the Ainsworth Strange Situation." In Greenberg, Mark T., Cicchetti, Dante, Cummings, E. Mark. *Attachment in the Preschool Years: Theory, Research, and Intervention.* Chicago: University of Chicago Press. pp. 121–160.

Bowlby, J. (1990). *A Secure Base: Parent-Child Attachment and Healthy Human Development.* Basic Books.

Effect of Vasectomies

Giovannucci, E., Tosteson, T. D., Speizer, F. E., Vessey, M. P., and Colditz, G. A. (1992). A long-term study of mortality in men who have undergone vasectomy. *New England Journal of Medicine*, *326*(21), 1392–1398.

Number of Siblings

Confluence Model Suggesting that Average Age of Household Is Key

Zajonc, R. B. (1976). Family configuration and intelligence: Variations in scholastic aptitude scores parallel trends in family size and the spacing of children. *Science 192*(4236), 227–236.

Debate over Possibility of No Effect

Guo, G., and Van Wey, L. K. (1999). Sibship size and intellectual development: Is the relationship causal? *American Sociological Review*, *64*(2), 169–187.

Phillips, M. (1999). Sibship size and academic achievement: What we now know and what we still need to know: Comment on Guo and VanWey. *American Sociological Review, 64*(2), 188–192.

Downey, D. B., Powell, B., Steelman, L. C., and Pribesh, S. (1999). Much ado about siblings: Change models, sibship size, and intellectual development: Comment on Guo and VanWey. *American Sociological Review, 64*(2), 193–198.

Guo, G., and Van Wey, L. K. (1999). The effects of closely spaced and widely spaced sibship size on intellectual development: Reply to Phillipas and to Downey et al. *American Sociological Review, 64*(2), 199–206.

Sex Mix Approach (showing effect)

Conley, D., and Glauber, R. (2006). Parental educational investment and children's academic risk estimates of the impact of sibship size and birth order from exogenous variation in fertility. *Journal of Human Resources, 41*(4), 722–737.

Twin Birth Approach (showing effect)

Cáceres-Delpiano, J. (2006). The impacts of family size on investment in child quality. *Journal of Human Resources, 41*(4), 738–754.

Possible Negative Effect of Only Child Status

Qian, N. (2009). *Quantity-quality and the one child policy: The only-child disadvantage in school enrollment in rural China* (No. w14973). National Bureau of Economic Research.

Refutation and Evidence That It Helped Economic Growth

Rosenzweig, M. R., and Zhang, J. (2009). Do population control policies induce more human capital investment? Twins, birth weight and

China's "one-child" policy. *The Review of Economic Studies*, *76*(3), 1149–1174.

Birth Spacing

Pettersson-Lidbom, P., and Skogman Thoursie, P. (2009). *Does child spacing affect children's outcomes? Evidence from a Swedish reform* (No. 2009: 7). Working paper//IFAU–Institute for Labour Market Policy Evaluation.

Impulse Control

Mischel, W., Ebbesen, E. B., and Raskoff Zeiss, A. (1972). Cognitive and attentional mechanisms in delay of gratification. *Journal of Personality and Social Psychology*, *21*(2), 204.

Mischel, W. (1974). Processes in delay of gratification. *Advances in Experimental social psychology*, *7*, 249–292.

Mischel, W., and Baker, N. (1975). Cognitive appraisals and transformations in delay behavior. *Journal of Personality and Social Psychology*, *31*(2), 254.

Moore, B., Mischel, W., and Zeiss, A. (1976). Comparative effects of the reward stimulus and its cognitive representation in voluntary delay. *Journal of Personality and Social Psychology*, *34*(3), 419.

Mischel, W., Shoda, Y., and Peake, P. K. (1988). The nature of adolescent competencies predicted by preschool delay of gratification. *Journal of Personality and Social Psychology*, *54*(4), 687.

Mischel, W., et al. (2011). "Willpower" over the life span: decomposing self-regulation. *Social Cognitive and Affective Neuroscience*, *6*(2), 252–256.

Effect of Odd Names

Houston, T. J., and Sumner, F. C. (1948). Measurement of neurotic tendency in women with uncommon given names. *The Journal of General Psychology, 39*(2), 289–292.

Hartman, A. A., Nicolay, R. C., and Hurley, J. (1968). Unique personal names as a social adjustment factor. *The Journal of Social Psychology, 75*(1), 107–110.

Joubert, C. E. (1983). Unusual names and academic achievement. *Psychological Reports, 53*(1), 266.

Zweigenhaft, R. L. (1977). The other side of unusual first names. *The Journal of Social Psychology, 103*(2), 291–302.

Zweigenhaft, R. L., Hayes, K. N., and Haagen, C. H. (1980). The psychological impact of names. *The Journal of Social Psychology, 110*(2), 203–210.

Anderson, T., and Schmitt, P. R. (1990). Unique first names in male and female psychiatric inpatients. *The Journal of Social Psychology, 130*(6), 835–837.

Pinzur, L., and Smith, G. (2009). First names and longevity. *Perceptual and motor skills, 108*(1), 149–160.

Effect of Black Names

Negative Effect

Bertrand, M., and Mullainathan, S. (2004). Are Emily and Greg more employable than Lakisha and Jamal? A field experiment on labor market discrimination. *The American Economic Review, 94*(4), 991–1013.

No Effect

Fryer, R. G., and Levitt, S. D. (2004). The causes and consequences of distinctively black names. *The Quarterly Journal of Economics*, *119*(3), 767–805.

(For effect of boys given feminine names see Schooling and the Hidden Curriculum, below.)

No Such Thing as Personality

Cantor, N., Mischel, W., and Schwartz, J. C. (1982). A prototype analysis of psychological situations. *Cognitive Psychology*, *14*(1), 45–77.

Shoda, Y., Mischel, W., and Wright, J. C. (1994). Intraindividual stability in the organization and patterning of behavior: Incorporating psychological situations into the idiographic analysis of personality. *Journal of Personality and Social Psychology*, *67*(4), 674.

Mischel, W., Mendoza-Denton, R., and Shoda, Y. (2002). Situation-behavior profiles as a locus of consistency in personality. *Current Directions in Psychological Science*, *11*(2), 50–54.

Class Differences in Word Exposure

Hart, Betty, and Risley, Todd R. (1995) *Meaningful differences in the Everyday Experience of Young American Children*. Baltimore: Paul H. Brookes Publishing.

Stay at Home Mothers—High v. Low Education Difference in Effects

Hsin, A. (2009). Parent's time with children: Does time matter for children's cognitive achievement?. *Social Indicators Research*, *93*(1), 123–126.

Phonics v. Whole Word

Thompson, G. B., McKay, M. F., Fletcher-Flinn, C. M., Connelly, V., Kaa, R. T., and Ewing, J. (2008). Do children who acquire word reading without explicit phonics employ compensatory learning? Issues of phonological recoding, lexical orthography, and fluency. *Reading and Writing, 21*(5), 505–537.

Thompson, G. B., Connelly, V., Fletcher-Flinn, C. M., and Hodson, S. J. (2009). The nature of skilled adult reading varies with type of instruction in childhood. *Memory & Cognition, 37*(2), 223–234.

Plow and Gender Roles

Alesina, A. F., Giuliano, P., and Nunn, N. (2011). *On the origins of gender roles: Women and the plough* (No. w17098). National Bureau of Economic Research.

Pre-Industrial Sleep Patterns

Ekirch, A. R. (2001). Sleep we have lost: Pre-industrial slumber in the British Isles. *American Historical Review, 106*(2), 343–386.

Goal Systems Theory

Shah, J., Higgins, T., and Friedman, R. S. (1998). Performance incentives and means: How regulatory focus influences goal attainment. *Journal of Personality and Social Psychology, 74*(2), 285.

Shah, J. Y., Kruglanski, A. W., and Friedman, R. (2003). Goal systems theory: Integrating the cognitive and motivational aspects of self-regulation. In Spencer, Steven J., Fein, Steven, Zanna, Mark P., and Olson, James M., eds., *Motivated social perception: The Ontario Symposium*, Vol. 9. Ontario symposium on personality and social psychology., (pp. 247–275). Mahwah, NJ: Lawrence Erlbaum Associates Publishers.

Kruglanski, A. W., Shah, J. Y., Fishbach, A., Friedman, R., Chun, W. Y., and Sleeth-Keppler, D. (2002). A theory of goal systems. *Advances in Experimental Social Psychology, 34*, 331–378.

Hyperbolic Discounting and Time Horizons

Laibson, D. (1997). Golden eggs and hyperbolic discounting. *The Quarterly Journal of Economics, 112*(2), 443–478.

Progresa/NYC Experiments

Molyneux, M. (2006). Mothers at the service of the new poverty agenda: Progresa/Oportunidades, Mexico's conditional transfer programme. *Social Policy & Administration, 40*(4), 425–449.

Behrman, J. R., Parker, S. W., and Todd, P. E. (2011). Do conditional cash transfers for schooling generate lasting benefits? A five-year follow-up of Progresa/Oportunidades. *Journal of Human Resources, 46*(1), 93–122.

Fryer Jr., R. G. (2010). *Financial incentives and student achievement: Evidence from randomized trials* (No. w15898). National Bureau of Economic Research.

Circumcision and HIV Transmission

Gray, R. H., et al. (2007). Male circumcision for HIV prevention in men in Rakai, Uganda: A randomised trial. *The Lancet, 369*(9562), 657–666.

Pets and Allergies

Perzanowski, Matthew S., Rönmark, Eva, Platts-Mills, Thomas A. E., and Lundbäck, Bo (2002). Effect of cat and dog ownership on sensitization and development of asthma among preteenage children *American Journal of Respiratory and Critical Care Medicine, 166*, 696–702.

Bacharier, L.B., et al. (2003). Pets and childhood asthma—how should the pediatrician respond to new information that pets may prevent asthma? *Pediatrics, 112,* 974–976.

Hygiene Hypothesis

Strachan, D. P. (1989). Hay fever, hygiene, and household size. *British Medical Journal, 299*(6710), 1259.

Folkerts, G., Walzl, G., Openshaw, P. J. (March 2000). Do common childhood infections 'teach' the immune system not to be allergic? *Immunology Today 21* (3): 118–20.

Bufford, J. D., Gern, J. E. (May 2005). The hygiene hypothesis revisited. *Immunology and Allergy Clinics of North America 25*(2): 247–62, v–vi.

Gibson, P. G., Henry, R. L., Shah, S., Powell, H., Wang, H. (2003). Migration to a western country increases asthma symptoms but not eosinophilic airway inflammation. *Pediatric Pulmonology 36*(3): 209–15.

Addo-Yobo, E. O., Woodcock, A., Allotey, A., Baffoe-Bonnie, B., Strachan D., Custovic A. (2007). Exercise-induced bronchospasm and atopy in Ghana: Two surveys ten years apart. *PLoS Medicine 4*(2): e70.

Aoyama, H., Hirata, T., Sakugawa, H., et al. (2007). An inverse relationship between autoimmune liver diseases and Strongyloides stercoralis infection. *The American Journal of Tropical Medicine and Hygiene 76*(5): 972–976.

Role of the Domestication of Animals in Western Economic Development

Diamond, Jared. (1997). *Guns, Germs and Steel: The Fates of Human Societies.* New York: W.W. Norton & Company, 14.

Discipline

Lareau, A. (2011). *Unequal Childhoods: Class, Race, and Family Life.* University of California Press.

Schooling and the Hidden Curriculum

Bowles, Samuel, and Herbert Gintis (1977). *Schooling in Capitalist America: Educational Reform and the Contradictions of Economic Life.* New York: Basic Books.

Coleman, J. S., Campbell, E. Q., Hobson, C. J., McPartland, J., Mood, A. M., Weinfeld, F. D., and York, R. L. 1966. *Equality of educational opportunity [summary report].* US Department of Health, Education, and Welfare, Office of Education.

Goffman, E. (1956). *The Presentation of Self in Everyday Life.* New York: Doubleday.

Willis, Paul (1977). *Learning to Labor: How Working Class Kids Get Working Class Jobs.* Farnham, U.K.: Gower Publishing Ltd.

(Class) Size Matters

Krueger, A. B., and Whitmore, D. M. (2001). The effect of attending a small class in the early grades on college—test taking and middle school test results: Evidence from Project STAR. *The Economic Journal, 111*(468), 1–28.

No Benefit to Private School

Krueger, A. B., and Zhu, P. (2004). Another look at the New York City school voucher experiment. *American Behavioral Scientist, 47*(5), 658–698.

No Benefit to Prestigious College Attendance for Non-poor Whites

Dale, S., and Krueger, A. B. (2011). *Estimating the return to college selectivity over the career using administrative earnings data* (No. w17159). National Bureau of Economic Research.

Dale, Stacy Berg, and Krueger, Alan B. (2002). Estimating the payoff of attending a more selective college: An application of selection on observables and unobservables. *Quarterly Journal of Economics, 107*(4 Nov.), 1491–1527.

Or High School Attendance

Abdulkadiroglu, A., Angrist, J. D., and Pathak, P. A. (2011). *The Elite Illusion: Achievement Effects at Boston and New York Exam Schools* (No. w17264). National Bureau of Economic Research.

Effect of Disruptive Peers

Figlio, D. N. (2007). Boys named Sue: Disruptive children and their peers. *Education Finance and Policy, 2*(4), 376–394.

Placebo Effect

Rosenthal, R., and Jacobson, L. (1968). *Pygmalion in the Classroom.* New York: Holt, Rinehart & Winston.

French, John R. P. (1950). "Field Experiments: Changing Group Productivity." in James G. Miller (ed.), *Experiments in Social Process: A Symposium on Social Psychology,* McGraw-Hill, 82.

Cobb, L. A., Thomas, G. I., Dillard, D. H., Merendino, K. A., Bruce, R. A. (May 1959). An evaluation of internal-mammary-artery ligation by a double-blind technic. *The New England Journal of Medicine 260*(22): 1115–1118.

Benson, H., and McCallie, D. P. (June 1979). Angina pectoris and the placebo effect. *The New England Journal of Medicine 300* (25): 1424–1429.

Moseley, J. B., O'Malley, K., Petersen, N. J., et al. (July 2002). A controlled trial of arthroscopic surgery for osteoarthritis of the knee. *The New England Journal of Medicine 347*(2): 81–88.

Lanotte, M., Lopiano, L., Torre, E., Bergamasco, B., Colloca, L., Benedetti, F. (November 2005). Expectation enhances autonomic responses to stimulation of the human subthalamic limbic region. *Brain, Behavior, and Immunity 19*(6): 500–509.

Depression/Placebo

Mayberg, H. S., Silva, J. A., Brannan, S. K., Tekell, J. L., Mahurin, R. K., McGinnis, S., Jerabek, P. A. (2002). The functional neuroanatomy of the placebo effect. *American Journal of Psychiatry 159* (5): 728–737.

Khan, A., Redding, N., Brown, W. A. (2008). The persistence of the placebo response in antidepressant clinical trials. *Journal of Psychiatric Research 42*(10): 791–796.

Kirsch, I., and Sapirstein, G. (1998) Listening to Prozac but hearing placebo: A meta-analysis of antidepressant medication. *Prevention & Treatment, 1,* ArtID 2a.

Kirsch, I., Deacon, B. J., Huedo-Medina, T. B., Scoboria, A., Moore, T. J., and Johnson, B. T. (2008). Initial severity and antidepressant benefits: A meta-analysis of data submitted to the Food and Drug Administration. *PLoS Medicine, 5*(2).

Fournier, J. C., DeRubeis, R. J., Hollon, S. D., Dimidjian, S., Amsterdam, J. D., Shelton R. C., et al. (2010). Antidepressant drug effects and depression severity: A patient-level meta-analysis. *Journal of the American Medical Association 303*(1): 47–53.

Bipolar

Sysko R., and Walsh, B. T. (2007). A systematic review of placebo response in studies of bipolar mania. *J Clin Psychiatry 68*(8): 1213–1217.

Anxiety

Schweizer, E., and Rickels, K. (1997). Placebo response in generalized anxiety: its effect on the outcome of clinical trials. *J Clin Psychiatry* *58* (Suppl 11): 30–8.

Piercy, M. A., Sramek, J. J., Kurtz, N.M., and Cutler, N. R. (1996). Placebo response in anxiety disorders. *The Annals of Pharmacotherapy, 30*(9): 1013–1019.

Speed/ADHD

Sandler, A. D., and Bodfish, J. W. (2008). Open-label use of placebos in the treatment of ADHD: A pilot study. *Child: Care, Health and Development, 34*(1): 104–110.

Volkow, N. D., Wang, G. J., Ma, Y., Fowler, J. S., Wong, C., Jayne, M., Telang, F., and Swanson, J.M. (2006). Effects of expectation on the brain metabolic responses to methylphenidate and to its placebo in non-drug abusing subjects. *Neuroimage 32*(4): 1782–1792.

Therapy works for ADHD

Fabiano, G. A., Pelham, W. E., Coles, E. K., Gnagy, E. M., Chronis-Tuscano, A., and O'Connor, B.C. (March 2009). A meta-analysis of behavioral treatments for attention-deficit/hyperactivity disorder. *Clinical Psychology Review 29*(2): 129–140.

Medication necessary for ADHD

Wigal, S. B. (2009). Efficacy and safety limitations of attention-deficit hyperactivity disorder pharmacotherapy in children and adults. *CNS Drugs 23* Suppl 1: 21–31.

Tolerance develops

Fusar-Poli, P., Rubia, K., Rossi, G., Sartori, G., and Balottin, U. (March 2012). Striatal dopamine transporter alterations in ADHD: Pathophysiology or adaptation to psychostimulants? A meta-analysis. *American Journal of Psychiatry, 169*(3): 264–272.

Lack of long-term studies

King, S., Griffin, S., and Hodges, Z. (July 2006). A systematic review and economic model of the effectiveness and cost-effectiveness of methylphenidate, dexamfetamine and atomoxetine for the treatment of attention deficit hyperactivity disorder in children and adolescents. *Health Technology Assessment 10*(23): iii–iv, xiii–146.
Greenhill, L. L., Posner, K., Vaughan, B. S., and Kratochvil, C. J. (April 2008). Attention deficit hyperactivity disorder in preschool children. *Child and Adolescent Psychiatric Clinics of North America 17*(2): 347–366, ix.

Medication lowers substance abuse risk

Faraone, S. V., and Wilens, T. E. (2007). Effect of stimulant medications for attention-deficit/hyperactivity disorder on later substance use and the potential for stimulant misuse, abuse, and diversion. *Journal of Clinical Psychiatry, 68* Suppl 11: 15–22.
Wilens, T. E., Faraone, S. V., Biederman, J., and Gunawardene, S. (January 2003). Does stimulant therapy of attention-deficit/hyperactivity disorder beget later substance abuse? A meta-analytic review of the literature. *Pediatrics 111*(1): 179–185.

Selective Attention and the Gorilla Test

Simons, D. J., and Chabris, C. F. (1999). Gorillas in our midst: Sustained inattentional blindness for dynamic events. *Perception-London, 28*(9), 1059–1074.

Divorce

Gruber, J. (2004). Is making divorce easier bad for children? The long-run implications of unilateral divorce. *Journal of Labor Economics*, *22*(4), 799–833.

Björklund, A., Ginther, D. K., and Sundström, M. (2007). Family structure and child outcomes in the USA and Sweden. *Journal of Population Economics*, *20*(1), 183–201.

Conley, D. (2004). *The Pecking Order: Which Siblings Succeed and Why*. New York: Pantheon.

Effect of Working Mom on Gender Equality in the Family

Conley, D. (2004). *The Pecking Order: Which Siblings Succeed and Why*. New York: Pantheon.

Sunny Day Effect on Stock Prices

Saunders, E. M. (1993). Stock prices and Wall Street weather. *The American Economic Review*, *83*(5), 1337–1345.

Hirshleifer, D., and Shumway, T. (2003). Good day sunshine: Stock returns and the weather. *The Journal of Finance*, *58*(3), 1009–1032.

Trombley, M. A. (1997). Stock prices and Wall Street Weather: Additional evidence. *Quarterly Journal of Business and Economics*, *36*(3), 11–21.

Effect Goes Away

Goetzmann, W. N., and Zhu, N. (2005). Rain or shine: Where is the weather effect? *European Financial Management*, *11*(5), 559–578.

McLean, R. D., and Pontiff, J. (2012). Does Academic Research Destroy Stock Return Predictability? Unpublished working paper. Boston College.

Parents' Influence on Smoking

Fagan, P., Brook, J. S., Rubenstone, E., and Zhang, C. (2005). Parental occupation, education, and smoking as predictors of offspring tobacco use in adulthood: A longitudinal study. *Addictive Behaviors*, *30*(3), 517–529.

Voting Behavior

Gerber, A. S., Green, D. P., and Shachar, R. (2003). Voting may be habit-forming: evidence from a randomized field experiment. *American Journal of Political Science*, *47*(3), 540–550.

Plutzer, E. (2002). Becoming a habitual voter: Inertia, resources, and growth in young adulthood. *American Political Science Review*, *96*(1), 41–56.

Verba, S., Schlozman, K. L., and Brady, H. E. (1995). *Voice and Equality: Civic Voluntarism in American Politics*. Harvard University Press.

Notes

Chapter 1. What *Not* to Expect When You're Expecting

1. There has since been a thirty-year follow-up on the administration of betamethasone on asthma rates complete with a placebo-administered group. There was apparently no deleterious effect. But that's just one outcome. Another study that looked at health and psychological functioning after twenty years also found no negative effect. However, a mouse study found decreased cognitive functioning, along with accelerated aging and increased mortality. And it may be the case that the human studies just haven't followed the subjects out long enough where the aging effects would manifest. I have yet to find a study that looked at the long-term effects of magnesium sulfate.

2. At least among stable troops of baboons. The problem, once again, in studying humans is that we can't be sure that the causation is not reversed, where it is the biological factors that lead to the different social positions—i.e. that folks who have a short cortisol spike aren't the ones who ascend the corporate hierarchy. But living among baboons, biologist Robert Sapolsky could blow a tranquilizer dart at the CEO baboon, thereby kidnapping him out of the mix and shaking up the hierarchy. He found that being higher in the pecking order *caused* lower cortisol levels—except when the hierarchy was unstable. In those situations—think the final days of Lehman Brothers or a turf war between gang leaders in west Baltimore—being at the top resulted in higher stress hormone levels.

3. Because you asked, cognitive tasks for mice are what you might expect: finding the cheese in the maze and other similar exercises. Emotional tests include one particularly cruel one meant to diagnose depression—aka "social defeat"—in which they put a mouse in a tank of water where there is an obscured Plexiglas platform in one spot, just below the surface. The mouse swims around the tank till she finds the platform and can rest on it while waiting for the lab helicopters to swoop in and rescue her. That's just the training. The actual test is that they switch things up so that there is actually no platform, as the mouse has come to expect. The measure of social defeat is how long the mouse swims until it tires out, gives up, and lets death wash over her. When she starts sinking, the graduate student scoops him out. Depressed mice give up earlier. And you thought the Navy SEALs had it tough!

4. I had to drill down into this finding, so I ran other analysis comparing identical twins. By comparing the birth weight differences between twins, one factors out a whole host of potentially confounding variables. For starters, they are genetically identical. So it's not like the birth weight difference is a result of one being a sickly mutant and one being robust—as could be the case with siblings. And what if the mother smoked crack during one pregnancy and ate only organic for the other one. It could be the crack effect causes both the low birth weight and the poor educational outcome, and the apparent relationship between gestational size and later measures is a statistical mirage. Identical twins fix that problem, too, since if the mother was a crackhead for one of them, she was for both of them. Really the only factor deciding which twin is the heavy one is random chance of who got the front row seat and got to hog all the placental resources. (It is actually possible for identical twins to have two placentae, but the same logic still holds: Due to random chance affecting uterine positioning, one gets more resources than the other.) I still found a significant birth weight effect even among identical twins. And I was not

alone. While my sociologist colleagues pretty much ignored my work—perhaps thinking, as one of my senior colleagues at Yale expressed, that research on biophysical factors like birth weight should be outside the purview of the field—economists latched on to it. Economists are always talking about natural "endowment"— by which they don't mean how well one is hung. They recognize that folks are born with a variety of innate potentials, and birth weight now gave them a quick and dirty way to measure this in their models. What followed over the next decade was a research literature that largely reinforced what I found in my 2000 paper (though as is their wont, many of the economists didn't cite my paper, which was published in a sociology journal). The effect held up in the United States but also in Sweden and a host of other countries. One study even demonstrated a robust correlation between average birth weight and the level of economic development in a given country.

5. Personally, I'm waiting for the Yom Kippur effect paper. Actually, Islam provides an exception to Ramadan fasting for pregnant women; however, some women may fast before they are aware they are with child or even after they know, just to be extra-pious.

6. But of course, they have to shoulder more weight of retirees. My father was born in one of the smallest birth cohorts of the twentieth century—1937. I, myself, was born in the middle of the steepest decline in birth rates (from 1960 to 1976): 1969. Evidently, only my parents (and a few other clueless folks) thought 1968—the year of the Tet offensive, three major assassinations (RFK, MLK, and Malcolm X), the disastrous Democratic convention hijacked in Chicago, and riots across urban America—was a good time to bring a child into the world. Of course, they did me a favor. And, I, in turn, did my own kids a favor by accidentally having them before the mini baby boom of the early 2000s. We had no problem, for example, finding a preschool, while others born just a few years later faced the notorious Harvard-level

competition (replete with spots for legacies, donors, and politically sensitive cases) in Manhattan preschool admissions. I'm hoping our luck lasts through college and grad school as well.

7. Where our lackadaisical roll of the pregnancy dice didn't turn up sevens was the specific months our kids were born. But I am fairly hopeful that—if indeed it is nutrition and not viral load that is driving this pattern—the ability to import fruits and vegetables from Chile in the dead of winter (not to mention our overabundance of food at any time of year) has pretty much wiped out this effect for recent birth cohorts. Fingers crossed. But I suppose I won't be around to find out—assuming I've done my parenting right and the kids outlive me.

8. Co-sleeping has been controversial ever since Americans became rich enough to afford separate bedrooms. I think Dr. Spock's advice reflected a general cultural obsession with preventing pedophilia. Puritan culture saw certain forms of physical contact between parent and child as deranged. By the mid-1970s, Dr. Richard Ferber was advocating the specific approach of allowing your baby to cry himself to sleep so that he learned to "self-soothe." Personally, I think Ferber's methodology caught on just because 1970s parents wanted to be able to ignore their kids once the sun went down so they could do drugs and swing. After all, what kind of decade needed public service announcements like this one?

Wife: Did you lock the kids in their room?
Husband: Huh?
Wife: Pass the damn joint already!

Chapter 2. Tying the Knot (and I Don't Mean Marriage— or the Umbilicus)

1. This "no effect" hypothesis got a huge boost in 1999 when Guang Guo and Leah van Wey published an article that examined test score changes over time when kids moved from smaller families to larger ones with the birth of younger siblings. They found that the increase in sibling number had no effect on their cognitive achievement. Thus, it may just be that parents who have lots of kids are simply not too bright. (I married into a family of ten kids, so I get to make such un-PC comments.) Then I came along, suspicious that this was the final word on the matter. (There were a number of limitations to the study that I won't go into.)

2. I had told myself that the effects of birth spacing are pretty small and could be entirely driven to the same selection effects of those who are able to plan reasonable birth intervals (and numbers of kids) and those, like Natalie and I, who have no clue what the heck we are doing. What we really need is to allow social scientists like me to randomly assign when certain study families get to have kids (and how many). In the meantime, a study that relied on a change in Swedish parental leave policy as the "treatment" to affect spacing found that, indeed, closer spacing was associated with poorer educational outcomes for kids. Argh!

Chapter 3. But Maybe You *Should* Name Your Boy Sue: What's Not in a Name

1. At birth, the scientific parent of means may also indulge in a couple other procedures. First, the Parentologist may want to collect fetal stem cells from the umbilical cord blood and store them in a cryobank (the same place they store frozen sperm). These cells have the capability of developing into any type of tissue and may someday come in handy if your kid (or possibly you, if you

match) needs an organ or some other form of regenerative medical treatment. Of course, medical science does not yet have the capability to grow a kidney in a petri dish, but it might by the time one of you needs it. But, of course, by then they may be able to reverse engineer any old cheek cell into a stem cell. So it's your call. Cell banking is expensive.

2. See http://www.youtube.com/watch?v=QX_oy9614HQ; I failed to test my kids at the appropriate age to see whether they would eat the marshmallow.

3. No less than James Heckman—2002 winner of the Nobel Prize in Economic Science—has gotten on the bandwagon, arguing that noncognitive skills like the ability to delay rewards, control impulses, focus for an extended period, and so forth are critical dimensions of child development and are, in large part, the root of class differences in achievement.

4. In case you think I'm pulling a James Frey here, check it out: http://www.nytimes.com/2003/09/25/nyregion/a-boy-named -yo-etc-name-changes-both-practical-and-fanciful-are-on-the -rise.html?scp=1&sq=a%20boy%20named%20Yo%20tara%20 bahrampour&st=cse.

5. See, for example: http://anthonybaxter.dreamwidth.org/51289 .html or "Right before the finish, comes the final insult: Knuckles. Yo Knuckles: sounds like that character from *Lilo and Stitch*, Cobra Bubbles, the government agent, to whom is addressed my favorite line in that movie: 'Oh good, my dog found the chain saw.'" (http://duckrabbit.blogspot.com/2005/05/freakonomy-in deed.html).

6. Yo was, in fact, born at Yale while we were teaching there.

Chapter 4. The Best Thesaurus Is a Human Thesaurus: How to Read to Your Kids

1. Perhaps because the Finns' language is so darn weird (with some fourteen declinations) that it's not even on the Indo-European language tree but is a linguistic freak along with Basque, Hungarian, Estonian, and (get this) Korean. I must admit that the link to Korean is debatable—or even doubtful. Most scholars think that the similarities are a result of the linguistic equivalent of convergent evolution—that is, they happened to take different paths from different roots to end up at a very similar place—sort of like bats and birds both having wings.

2. His handwriting, meanwhile, is still atrocious; but I didn't worry about that since we type everything these days anyway. Along with penmanship, the list of neglectable skills includes music and sports. Of course, sports are good to do for exercise and fun. And if music gives your kids pleasure, then by all means, strum away. . . . But when we are talking about economic success and security, they are bad roads to go down in the hopes of "making it." There are very few jobs as professional musicians or athletes. And even if you do "make it," your professional career is likely to be a few years long at most, in sports, at least.

   For example, to take my sport of choice: There are 64,000 registered boxers in the world. Only 10 make a million dollars or more. There are 28 teams in the N.B.A.; they each have a roster of 15 players. That's 420 professional positions in this country in basketball. There are 30 football teams with a good 60 players each. That's 1,800 positions (with one of the shortest average career spans of any profession, I might add). I don't know the statistics for concert violinists and the like, but I think you get the picture. Music and sports both represent what the economist Robert Frank likes to call "winner-take-all markets." Basically, what this means is that there are incredibly high rewards in such a field—but only for one or a few workers—leaving the rest of the industry's aspirants to hold on to their day jobs. At one time, there was good money to be made as a trumpet player since every small city (and even many large towns) had its own orchestra. But with the advent of transportation like the car, so that folks can drive to the nearest major city to see a more prestigious orchestra, and more important, with the advent of recorded music, those jobs fell away. After all, if you can listen to Yo-Yo Ma on iTunes for the same price as any other cellist, why would you settle for second best? (Well, I personally would not be able to tell the difference.) So Yo-Yo Ma becomes a multimillionaire and all the other cellists are shit out of luck. Same dynamic holds for many other industries besides sports and music, including fashion, architecture, and even corporate management.

That said, if my kids wanted to pursue a career in a winner-take-all market and devoted themselves to it, of course I would be supportive. I'm a Western parent, after all, and we value individuality. If singing or acting or painting is their God-chosen vocation, then I will come to all their performances to cheer them on; oh, and I will make sure to leave them a big tip when I come to eat where they are waiting tables. Luckily, they have almost no athletic talent. I took care of that by passing on one of my two mutant, nonfunctional, alpha-actinin-3 protein fast-twitch muscle genes—though they each got one of the good sprinter genes from their mother, who is quite the athlete, and who has two copies to pass on. They aren't bad in music, but don't seem to practice much. They do like art, creative writing, and acting. But I figure at least the latter two of those options are generalizable skills. They won't necessarily end up as starving poets if they are good writers (hence my focus on reading and writing); and as for acting—God, I hate actors, but I suppose being able to make decent oral presentations and being comfortable on stage is going to be important. So hopefully the acting has a positive spillover effect there.

3. But an unanticipated, collateral benefit of bearing children was that I never again had trouble falling asleep despite occasional bouts of preparental insomnia. And even if I did encounter a bump or two on the road to Snoozeville, I didn't really get all worked up about it because I knew that I could survive on no sleep for extended periods—if need be. In fact, like many parents, it's now impossible for me to sleep through an entire night in one chunk, even when I am away from my kids and noisy pets at some luxury hotel. I always get up sometime in the so-called wee hours and read or do email for a while. And then sure enough, I will drift back off for my second round of REM. I later read an article about how peasants lived in Britain a couple hundred years ago: They would basically hibernate during the cold winters, huddling together and sleeping for most of the hours of the day, waking occasionally to nibble on some stale bread. The author explained that before electric lighting, most people slept in two cycles. Peasants would fall asleep shortly after the sun went down; adults, at least, would wake in the middle of the night for pillow talk (with or without candlelight) and hanky-panky before drifting off to sleep again. Most folks didn't know how to read, so that wasn't an option; hence the high fertility rates of preindustrial societies despite the fact that multiple generations slept in the same bed—or on the same dirt floor if you were a English peasant.

4. Yes, other than reading each book to both of them, I haven't figured out how to break down their gender-stereotyped preferences in literature quite yet. I blame that on the plow; yes, you heard right, the plow. Before the plow was invented, the mode of agriculture was tilling the soil with a hoe. Some societies adopted plowing if they had large domesticatable beasts to pull the damn thing. Others stuck to the solely human approach, since it was pretty hard to get a lion, hippo, or zebra to pull anything. The key, however, is that while both men and women could and did hoe (or ho, for that matter), plows required upper body strength and

thus led to a gender-based division of labor where the men did the sowing of the seed (so to speak) and the women tended to other tasks. Some economists (yes, economists study literally everything these days), claim that this ancient technological difference can still explain gender inequality today. Communities that plowed millennia ago tend to be more traditionalistic when it comes to sex roles, and those that hoed are more egalitarian—all the way up through and including the age of the internet. Who knows how this study will stand up to replication, but I personally like any social science that involves hoes, large beasts, and upper body strength.

5. Or take Italian, which betrays how primitive the country was just a hundred or so years ago when much of the modern world was invented. Instead of a separate word for "camera" or "typewriter" or "car," they call them all machines (*macchina*: pronounced **mack**-een-a). So instead of typing, you "hit the machine"; but hopefully you don't "hit the machine" when you are driving your car or taking a photo.

Chapter 5. Practicing the Delicate Arts of Extortion and Bribery (How *Else* Are American Children Supposed to Catch Up to the Finnish People in Math?)

1. It is a rather sad story, actually. Aleksandr Khazanov suffered from depression and went missing in June 2001, later to be found dead.

2. Only problem was that E didn't actually know the days of the week or the months of the year. At least not in their proper order. She was constantly asking how far away a particular event was if I said it was on Sunday. Likewise, she had no idea whether her birthday (January) was near or far. At first I didn't worry. I rationalized that Albert Einstein didn't know his own phone number. I told this trivia to E to make her feel better for not remembering

the order of the months. "When asked why not, Einstein responded, 'Why should I memorize something that I can look up in any telephone book.' And he's a genius, or so they say." They asked if he really wasn't a genius, given my snarky tone and aside at the end of my explanation. I assured them that he actually was, but that science didn't work that way. One brilliant lone wolf didn't just think up inventions, make discoveries, or formulate theories from scratch in the dark but, rather, that everyone borrows and tinkers and threads together lots of existing material to make something novel, that we all stand on the shoulders of giants in Newton's famous phrase and that "genius" was a so-called social construction. But later, of course, I realized that E wouldn't have been able to even look up her phone number in a phone book since she didn't know alphabetical order. So it was time for some memorization. We started with our home address and phone number in case of emergency. Then we moved on to the alphabet song, kind of embarrassing to sing with a seven-year-old.

3. And yet the circumcision battle was one I lost with respect to Yo because at the time of his birth I couldn't produce any research proving its health benefits. (We should have trusted the Jews and Muslims.) He had been born in that decade-long window when the children of educated Americans had just abandoned the practice as "barbaric" but before the African-based AIDS transmission research had been conducted. Now scientists know that the Langerhorn cells on the bottom of the penis tip die if not protected by a foreskin, and it is these cells that receive and transmit viruses ranging from HIV to human papilloma virus (HPV), which has been implicated in cervical cancer among women. So not only does being circumcised make you last longer during sex (by dulling some of the sensation through everyday friction as compared to a sheathed penis), it can help your lady friend avoid genital warts and cancer. (And it can even help males avoid throat cancer

from oral sex on either men or women.) With all this in mind (but forgetting my Freud), I explained this research to eleven-year-old Yo and offered him a hundred dollars if he would agree to be circumcised. He refused and didn't even counter with a higher figure, as is usually his habit. Evidently, even for Yo some things are priceless.

Chapter 6. GET THEM THE PUPPY! GET THEM THE PUPPY!

1. My absolute all-time favorite pet! We rescued the bullfrog from being sold as food in a Chinatown supermarket. Not only does he live outside our back window in the rain gutter, he doesn't require food because—this is the best part—he just eats insects that would otherwise be biting us! I think I love him. We got E to kiss him once to see if he'd turn into a prince. No zoonosis was reported.

2. These were drunk because Natalie had done some sort of art-science experiment where she raised wild mice she captured on offerings of Prozac-infused water, vodka, and sugar water. Like the experimenter herself, they all preferred the vodka.

3. Many modern, progressive parents seek to do everything naturally. Even back in my undergraduate days at Berkeley, the motto with respect to drugs was, "If it's organic, don't panic." Never mind that most synthetic drugs are organic in the technical sense of being carbon-based compounds. What they meant was that magic mushrooms and marijuana were safe since they grew out of the ground, but you should worry about impurities and the risk of overdosing when it came to LSD, cocaine, methamphetamines, or anything else cooked up in some chemistry major's basement. This is probably a pretty good rule of thumb not just for recreational drugs, but for food consumption as well. Many folks in my demographic take it a little too far, however.

   Hemlock, tobacco, snakebites, and rape are natural, but most of us would like to put them in the same class as sodium cyanide.

And if we're really going to go natural—like the caveman diet that recommends eating only raw stuff that can be hunted or gathered—we should expect most of our children to die and prepare to live about fifty-five years max, since that was the outer reaches of the human lifespan in the good old days before we "unnaturally" domesticated wild crops ~10,000 years ago. What's more, we would be hacking each other to death at rates that would make the South Bronx in the late 1970s seem like a pacifist meditation retreat. And how is a "naturally" illiterate, feral kid going to succeed in the knowledge economy with his language of grunts and snorts? But who can blame us confused religious mutts for looking for some guidance through the thicket of choices contemporary society offers us? Best, perhaps, to pick and choose from the natural ideology. Breast-feeding is good—if possible. Illiteracy bad. I think vaccines are a helluva invention as are antibiotics (if used sparingly). Antibiotics, in fact, made this book possible by saving my life when I was struck with spinal meningitis at two weeks of age. So forgive me, fellow Berkeley alums, for liking modern, artificial medicine.

Some people even seek "natural" sexual and social guidelines from our primate cousins with respect to the question of monogamy. Among primates, polygamy is predicted by sexual dimorphic body size—i.e. the difference in average body size between the male and female sexes. Gorillas, where one dominant male mates with many females, have a male-to-female body ratio of 1.5. Male gibbons, who make good (faithful) husbands and fathers, are only 1.02 times as big as their wives on average. Where are we? Somewhere in the middle at 1.1 (other species with a ratio of 1.2 are polygamous). So, no answer there. Go figure. Comparative primate genetics is also little help in guiding human behavioral norms. Our second closest relatives, bonobos, are peaceful, horny orgiasts while chimpanzees are highly violent (and constitute the species most related to us).

4. Even worms (*Helminths*) may not be so bad. Evidently, they co-evolved symbiotically with us, and when children are dewormed, they are at greater risk for allergies and GI problems such as inflammatory bowel disease (IBD). Besides, if they are eating your food, they keep you nice and trim—now there's a weight-loss marketing opportunity!
5. South America had the llama (and its cousin, the alpaca). Australia had giant wombats and other species that might have been domesticatable had they coevolved with humans. But alas, having not encountered humans till so late in prehistory (circa 50,000 years ago), they had no natural fear of them and their spears and thus were rendered extinct almost immediately. The survivors of this pogrom were, by definition, not very domesticatable since they tended to be skittish and need large open spaces (e.g., kangaroos). Though some have argued that rather than importing sheep and cattle, which have taken a huge toll on the fragile ecosystem of the island, the British should have farmed wombat, echidna, and kangaroo meat. These endemic species don't devour the root systems of the Australian grasses and thus don't ruin the thin topsoil of this driest, oldest continent. Africans, meanwhile, might have been able to hitch a plow to an elephant, but the animals reproduce too slowly (and not very well in captivity), making them a losing proposition as a farming investment. Zebras, meanwhile, are bad-asses who won't kowtow to no one (as they need to be to survive the predatory environment of the savannah).
6. Domestication is really a two-way street. Wolves/dogs trained us as well, circling our dinner tables. Like paying off the mafia, we threw scraps to some, and eventually, we bought off ones who served as protection against their more feral cousins.
7. This as a technique was riskier than inoculation (which it preceded). The practice originated in China and India and was brought to the West by Lady Mary Wortley Montagu, who was the wife of the British ambassador to the Ottoman Empire and

observed variolation in what would be modern-day Turkey. Of course, being a woman, she gets few kudos in the annals of immunology.

8. Okay, so maybe we went too far with the bats and the monkey, which, I later learned, are two of the greats fonts of zoonotic disease transfer to humans. The Nipah virus, for example, came to humans courtesy of fruit bats, the very species we kept, also known as flying foxes. And, of course, our simian cousins (though not this species in particular, the long-tailed macaque) were the origin of HIV. So maybe a good rule is to stick with pets that have coevolved with humans so that we've already swapped germs back and forth over hundreds of years of evolution so as to avoid any immunological surprises.

9. Of course, from the plague to bird flu, coexisting with animals has also been the source of deadly epidemics. But even these may have contributed to European good fortune, ultimately. Take the black death, for instance. European populations developed a level of immunity to the plague that other peoples did not share, so it was the fleas on the rats aboard the ships that landed in Montezuma's empire that committed most of the genocide of native peoples, thereby clearing the way for European settlement. This was probably at least as critical as the superior arms that the whites possessed. Second, those military technologies themselves were perhaps indirectly a result of the very same pestilence. One theory holds that the Renaissance was at least partly attributable to the massive population reductions that preceded it. Throughout history, after major wars, boom periods have typically followed (think the 1950s, for example). Ditto for epidemics (e.g., the Roaring '20s after the flu pandemic of 1918). The loss of a third to half of the European population from bubonic plague in the fourteenth century meant that the survivors had increased wealth per capita and, perhaps more importantly, the entire feudal social structure was upended (at least

temporarily). (Growing populations are often associated with progress, but they may be effect and not cause.) Think of modern society as the postmigraine high after the miserably sick period of the Middle Ages. Or, as an alternative theory holds, perhaps it was accelerating trade along the Silk Road that caused the black death *and* the Renaissance. Whether or not the plague helped cause the Renaissance, we might have sidestepped the Holocaust had we avoided the disease five centuries earlier. Though the roots of anti-Semitism precede the black death, certainly the plague didn't help the PR case of European Jews, since they were overrepresented among the traders whom the infected rat vectors accompanied back from Asia. While Jews were targeted for retribution, it really does take a village to create an epidemic: had the Catholic Church not gone on an anticat crusade (thinking the felines were manifestations of Satan), the whole thing could have been avoided since we would not have been overrun by infected rats in the first place. So the point of the story is not that the plague was ultimately good or bad (or that Jews or Catholics were to blame), but that the animals with whom we know and live protect us against the invasive species we don't.

Chapter 7. Shut the F* Up, Dad! Discipline (or Lack Thereof)

1. I tell myself that I'm a sociologist and hence am going into these four-day retreats for anthropological reasons. So, a few observations are in order: The French elites all know each other. Perhaps this is due to the fact that France is a much smaller country, but I tend to doubt that, since many of the Chinese also seemed to have known each other well before our four days in Seattle. Rather, I think it was the structure of their educational systems where the future elites are identified at a very young age and channeled into special schools. (In France these are the *grandes écoles*.) By contrast, among the Spartan-like Americans, there was a high representation

of military officers who had graduated from the academies (people I enjoyed meeting, since before I did all these programs I had almost no exposure to the military growing up in a liberal, artistic household in New York City—except for an aborted enrollment in ROTC during college). But these weren't what I imagine were typical military officers. They all had graduate degrees from places like the University of Chicago in addition to their training at the National War College. There were also a remarkable number of Rhodes (and Marshall) scholars among both the military and non-military fellows alike. In fact, I was one of the only members to have graduated from a public college (granted, it was Berkeley, but that said, I didn't even know what a Rhodes was when I graduated with my 2.98 GPA . . .). Oh, and there were a number of blacks among the American group (mostly from the military side—and almost no Latinos for some strange reason), and there were almost no ethnic minorities represented among the other countries' delegations.

2. Okay, okay, so maybe sports have some utility after all.

Chapter 8. Turn Your Feral Child into a Nice American Capitalist (You Know You Want To)

1. Though it is equally possible that Sue was not the one who started up being disruptive but rather that he was picked on by other kids and got into trouble in response to such maltreatment by peers. This is a challenge that economist Charles Manski calls "the reflection problem" that plagues peer and social network research—namely, when behavior is endogenous to a network of social actors, it's basically impossible to parcel out "who started it" (as sniping siblings might put it).

2. I had thought the critical period for attendance was the first half of fifth grade, but evidently the bureaucrats had just changed that unbeknownst to me.

3. Natalie, I might explain, belongs to a web-based network called "pigeon911"; this listserv posts all-points bulletins about injured birds (sparrows and swallows in addition to the infamous rock dove), and whoever is nearest the avian in distress is expected to swoop down and collect it before a hawk or pigeon-hating human does.

4. But on the other hand, what do I know? I scored a 119 on the test to get into Stuyvesant when the cutoff for that year was 120. I should have been on the other side of the line in the MIT study, but since I lived in a poor school district, I was able to go to summer school to make up the point. (You can read all about this if you're willing to read yet another of my memoirs, *Honky*, about growing up in a Puerto Rican and black neighborhood of housing projects.) I don't know what Eugene scored, but I'm sure it was better than my score.

5. Doctoral students are generally not expected to pay for their degree. In fact, they receive free tuition and a stipend for working as a research or teaching assistant.

6. Learned from Wild Man Steve Brill during an instructional tour that Natalie dragged us on. See: http://www.wildmanstevebrill.com/.

Chapter 9. If It's Organic, Don't Panic—and Other Tips I Learned in Berkeley for Drugging One's Kids

1. In actuality, his only disability—if you could call it that—was a lisp. He was unable to pronounce the letter "s" properly. He did fine in school and, in fact, won the 1953 Nobel Prize in Literature (one of the "real" Nobels).

2. He is famous for having fallen in love with his own work of art. He asked a favor of Venus, who did him the solid one of turning the sculpture into a real woman. Evidently, the play version of the classic Greek tale, *Pygmalion*, was popular in London during the

time of George Bernard Shaw and inspired him to pen his own modern adaptation where he told the story of Eliza Doolittle and the efforts of Henry Higgins to win a bet by turning her into a lady of sorts. Fast-forward to 1964, and *Pygmalion* had morphed into the musical *My Fair Lady*, which made it from stage to the big screen, starring the inimitable Audrey Hepburn, winning eight Academy Awards.

3. All the kids improved. Among first graders, the "treated" kids improved 27 points and the control group 12 points. The difference for second graders was 10 points and basically declined to nothing after that. So our concern for Yo getting stigmatized back in first grade was not unfounded. Though, on the other hand, it is not necessarily the case that the effect is symmetrical, meaning negative preconceptions have the same magnitude of impact in the opposite direction. Nor is it clear that the same effect demonstrated in the 1960s would continue to hold fifty years later when the awe for science and (social) scientists may have diminished. See page 75 of *Pygmalion in the Classroom*.

4. The Pygmalion study took place in the good old days before university institutional review boards put an end to all the fun by preventing devious experiments like this. This study was one of a handful of brilliant—if twisted—experiments that, in fact, catalyzed the movement for greater protections of human subjects in social science experiments. You could call it our "Tuskegee moment." Not only were there the Milgram electric shock experiments, but Craig Haney and Philip Zimbardo locked Stanford undergraduates into a fake prison in the basement of the psychology building and randomly assigned them to be either guards or prisoners to demonstrate the power of social roles on behavior. (It got so out of control, in fact, that they had to abort the experiment partway through.) Ah, the good old days. Now, the best we can do is ask a bunch of survey questions (so boring!) or wear a gorilla suit.

This experiment in selective attention received the glorious "Ig-Nobel Prize" for showing what idiots we can be. E and I failed it. Yo and Natalie passed (i.e. noticed the gorilla), which led me to ask Christopher Chabris (the mad scientist behind it all) whether it might be used as a diagnostic for ADD. Of course, now I've ruined it for you, but feel free to try it on your kids. The video works best on a big screen—Google "selective attention test" or "gorilla test." *Simons, D. J., & Chabris, C. F. (1999). Gorillas in our midst: Sustained inattentional blindness for dynamic events. Perception, 28, 1059–1074.*

5. Americans get way too many omega-6 long-chain fatty acids in our diet. These promote inflammation (which is necessary for responses to damage, stress, infection, and so on). We don't get enough omega-3s or omega-9s. Abundant in fish oils, omega-3s are anti-inflammatory, and since inflammation plays a role in many chronic diseases (including cardiovascular disease and potentially conditions related to brain function), balancing our intake with omega-3 supplements seems in order, even though long-term studies don't show reduced mortality risk. (Omega-9s come from almonds, which I also force on my kids, and also reduce the risk of heart disease.)

6. That possibility—understandably—scared the daylights out of me. The four As of schizophrenia diagnosis are flat Affect; Auditory

hallucination (i.e. that voice inside your head telling you to kill the president); Alliteration (speaking in poetry, essentially); and Associative thinking (everything's connected, hence the tendency toward paranoia).

7. Okay, I hope the prohibition against French fries and soda is fairly self-evident. But I feel like I might need to explain why juice is also verboten. Juice is basically water plus fructose. Fructose is the absolutely worst kind of sugar one can consume. While glucose is metabolized in every cell in the body, fructose is only processed by the liver and results in not only animal starch (glycogen) but also dangerous triglycerides. But wait, you say, fructose comes from fruit, and fruit is good for you! The fiber in fruit is what's good for you. When you drink a glass of orange juice, you are getting the sugar from a whole bunch of oranges with almost none of the fiber (even if you get the version with lots of pulp). Fructose is nature's way to get you to eat the fiber (and to egest the seeds [which is the real purpose of fruit from the plant's point of view—dispersal]). (Natalie always eats the seeds when she eats fruit, claiming that she needs to uphold her end of the bargain with the tree or bush— never mind that given we live in New York, I highly doubt that any seed she egests actually sprouts a new plant.) And while we are on the topic, sucrose (i.e. natural cane sugar) is no better than high-fructose corn syrup (HFCS) since HFCS is just a combo of fructose and glucose; sucrose, meanwhile, is just the chemical combination of fructose and glucose, which is cleaved apart first thing upon digestion. Gatorade used to be sweetened by glucose and it tasted rather rotten, but it helped your working muscles immediately. Then PepsiCo bought it from the University of Florida and switched the sugar to HFCS. Now it's lost its purpose and is not much healthier than Pepsi itself.

8. I was curious as to how this drug worked, so under the guise of not giving my children anything that I wasn't willing to experiment with on myself (yes, a ridiculous rationale I know), I decided

to try his pills one day. I wondered if perhaps I was still ADD myself and whether my mother should have agreed to have me take Ritalin back in the 1970s. At the very least, I figured I'd enjoy a very successful day of focused writing. Boy was I wrong. In the end, I got no writing done and instead spent the entire time at my office surfing eBay. And whereas I truly did need to buy a pair of speakers for my house, I certainly didn't need five pairs of speakers. But I simply couldn't stop myself from bidding, and then like magic, a still better pair would appear just after I'd confirmed the last bid. So now I am the not-so-proud owner of four (out of five auctions) pairs of vintage 1960s speakers.

9. Of course, there is such a thing: coca leaves from Bolivia. But the DEA might have a thing or two to say about that.

Chapter 10. Go Ahead and Get Divorced—Your Kids' Genes Will Never Notice

1. Males can have literally thousands of offspring if they are at the top of the pecking order, so to speak, but they can also end up not reproducing at all if they end up at the bottom. Females, meanwhile, have a physical cap of how many children they can bear in a lifetime but can generally reproduce if they so desire.

2. A study about the effect of studies found that two-thirds of the effect was dissipated by the publication of a research paper documenting it. The new research that this study spawned, in turn, was to try to answer the question of why effects weren't 100 percent reduced in financial markets since they are supposed to be efficient at taking advantage of any and all new information.

3. Just to be on the safe side, we haven't ever had a television in our house, but then this little thing called the internet fouled everything up, since my kids manage to find every show they want to watch on some website or another. So I decided to require them to walk on a treadmill or pedal a stationary bike while they are

watching. No, I can't be 100 percent sure that this is an adequate solution (or that watching *Family Guy* is bad for them in the first place), but I'm probably not doing any harm by making them exercise while consuming the idiot box (or, rather, laptop). The treadmill plan was arrived at with the kids themselves, after we discussed the potentially negative (and in their argument, the positive) effects of television. It was a compromise, and that very process of negotiation is part of the overall parenting strategy. Now they can articulate the pros and cons and fit their own experience within a broader set of goals and scientific literature. It was what others would call a "teachable moment"—except for the fact that it is ongoing (and thus not a moment), and it wasn't me teaching them, it was us researching the issue together. But, of course, I will still keep a vigilant eye out for any changes in their reading behavior, their physical development, and their academic performance. I will fine-tune the plan accordingly. Maybe I will reduce the amount of time they can watch—or raise it, but tie the increase explicitly to other inputs (such as reading time) or outputs (such as their test scores). In other words, a scientific parent's work is never done. The experiment never ends. The truth is that your job as a parent is never done until you are on your deathbed at a ripe old age, and your kids are not. Sure, there are markers along the way, signposts of success: we'd like them to survive early childhood relatively intact with ten fingers and toes and knowing how to read; we would like our kids to graduate high school with decent grades and friendships and without a drug habit. Most middle-class American parents want their offspring to obtain a BA (at least). And we'd like them not to have to move back in with us during their twenties (or god forbid, their thirties or forties). We'd like them to form stable romantic relationships with healthy folks and to bear us grandchildren. The rest, as they say, is probably rounding error.

4. At least as measured by Olympic medals per capita, which is as

good a measure for cross-cultural sports comparisons as there is, I suppose.

5. Her parents decided she was too young to have a boyfriend. I had no clue at the time that she was the daughter of Depeche Mode's lead singer and thus didn't get my tuition's worth in 1980s nostalgic name-dropping among my high school friends.

6. And folks wonder why my generation is messed up? This was what was piped into our brains as developmentally vulnerable toddlers. (And this was educational programming paid for by our tax dollars!)

7. That said, it's probably not the best idea for a five-year-old to take advice from a pimp-looking dude who talks to young boys anyway.

8. Technically, if their genetic similarity in looks is causing the twins to be confused and/or treated way more similarly, then that is an effect of genes and thus should unproblematically be part of the overall "genetic" effect. However, this flies in the face of commonsense understandings of what we mean by genetic effects, and, as mentioned in the main text, makes the estimates less externally valid to the rest of us. However, the increased cross-sibling interaction that may make them turn out more similar is another story—that's just plain biasing of results.

9. Never mind for the moment that now that geneticists can search across the genome for the actual variation that correlates with these outcomes, they can find only a small fraction of it. This mystery of the remaining "missing heritability" is one of the hottest topics in human genetics these days. One theory has that a good portion of the genetic component of everything from height to IQ is due to so-called "rare" alleles that we will only discover when we have fully sequenced thousands of individuals—that is, not just test for the half million or so markers that span the genome in typical "chips" but actually read every one of the three billion base pairs in the human genome. This is the goal of endeavors

such as NIH's 1000 Genomes Project, which will also help answer the question of whether it is genetic "dark matter"—i.e. what was once thought to be junk DNA between genes—that explains heritability. And yet another theory is that we actually inherit environmentally inscribed, epigenetic marks that contribute to what appear to be genetic differences at first blush. This is known as neo-Lamarckianism, so named after the once disgraced (but now resuscitated) Jean-Baptiste Lamarck, who famously argued that the giraffe's neck evolved through stretching efforts, the fruits of which were passed on to the next generation, and so on . . . While all these theories are sexy, as more progress is made, it seems that the "missing heritability" has been hiding in plain sight—that is, that traits like body mass index or depression are affected by hundreds if not thousands of alleles that each have effects so small that they don't pop up when we statistically examine them one by one but which together can actually account for the "expected" genetic components of those outcomes.

10. The company now does report this test of which James Watson (of DNA discovery fame) himself refused to hear his results.

About the Author

DALTON CONLEY is University Professor and Professor of Sociology, Medicine, and Public Policy at New York University. He also serves as a Research Associate at the National Bureau of Economic Research (NBER). In a pro bono capacity, he is Dean of Arts and Sciences for the University of the People (UoPeople)—a tuition-free institution committed to expanding access to higher education. He has previously served as Dean for the Social Sciences and Chair of Sociology at NYU and is currently Chair of the Children and Youth Section of the American Sociological Association. In 2005, Conley was the first sociologist to win the National Science Foundation's Alan T. Waterman Award, given annually to one outstanding young scientist in any field of math, science, or engineering. He is also a 2011 Guggenheim Fellow. He lives in New York City with his two children and many animals.